The Creative Curriculum® for Infants, Toddlers & Twos
Second Edition, Revised

Volume 2: Routines and Experiences

Diane Trister Dodge
Sherrie Rudick
Kai-leé Berke

Contributing Authors: Donna Bloomer, Laura J. Colker,
Amy Laura Dombro, and Diane Woodard

TeachingStrategies® · Washington, D.C.

Editors: Toni Bickart and Laurie Taub
Cover design: Abner Nieves
Interior illustrations: Jennifer Barrett O'Connell
Layout/production: Jeff Cross

The drawings of toys, equipment, and furniture on pages 203, 224, and 232 are based on products offered by Community Playthings.

The drawings of toys, equipment, and furniture on pages 326 and 374 are based on products offered by Kaplan Early Learning Company.

The drawing of toys, equipment, and furniture on page 360 is based on products offered by Lakeshore Learning Materials.

Teaching Strategies, Inc.
P.O. Box 42243
Washington, DC 20015
www.TeachingStrategies.com
ISBN: 978-1-60617-416-6

Teaching Strategies and *The Creative Curriculum* names and logos are registered trademarks of Teaching Strategies, Inc., Washington, D.C. Brand-name products of other companies are suggested for illustrative purposes and are not required for implementation of the curriculum.

Library of Congress Cataloging-in-Publication Data

Dodge, Diane Trister.
    The creative curriculum for infants, toddlers & twos / Diane Trister Dodge, Sherrie Rudick, Kai-leé Berke ; Donna Bloomer ... [et al.], contributing authors. -- 2nd ed., rev.
        p. cm.
    ISBN 978-1-60617-415-9 (v. 1) -- ISBN 978-1-60617-416-6 (v. 2) -- ISBN 978-1-60617-417-3 (v. 3)
    1. Education, Preschool--Curricula--United States. 2. Child care--United States. 3. Curriculum planning--United States. 4. Child development--United States. I. Rudick, Sherrie. II. Berke, Kai-leé. III. Title.

    LB1140.4.D632 2011
    372.19--dc22
                                2010038683

Printed and bound in the United States of America
2015   2014   2013   2012   2011
10 9 8 7 6 5 4 3 2

Contents

Volume 1: The Foundation 1–186

Volume 2: Routines and Experiences
Part A: Routines 187

Chapter 6: Hellos and Good-Byes 188

Supporting Development and Learning 190

Creating an Environment for Hellos and Good-Byes 191

Caring and Teaching. 192
Supporting Children and Families During Hellos and Good-Byes   192
Supporting Children Emotionally Throughout the Day   194
Responding to What Children Need   195

Sharing Thoughts About Hellos and Good-Byes 199

Chapter 7: Diapering and Toileting 200

Supporting Development and Learning 202

Creating an Environment for Diapering and Toileting 203
The Diaper-Changing Station   203
The Toileting Area   204

Caring and Teaching. 205
Keeping Children Safe and Healthy   205
Responding to What Children Need   206
Working in Partnership With Families   212

Sharing Thoughts About Diapering and Toileting 213

Chapter 8: Eating and Mealtimes 214

Supporting Development and Learning 216

Creating an Environment for Eating and Mealtimes 217

Caring and Teaching. 218
Keeping Children Safe and Healthy   220
Responding to What Children Need   221
Working in Partnership With Families   226

Sharing Thoughts About Eating and Mealtimes. 227

Chapter 9: Sleeping and Nap Time 228

Supporting Development and Learning 230

Creating an Environment for Sleeping and Nap Time 231

Caring and Teaching. 234
Responding to What Children Need   237
Working in Partnership With Families   240

Sharing Thoughts About Sleeping and Nap Time 241

Chapter 10: Getting Dressed 242

Supporting Development and Learning 244

Creating an Environment for Getting Dressed. 245

Caring and Teaching 246
Responding to What Children Need   249
Working in Partnership With Families   252

Sharing Thoughts About Getting Dressed 253

Part B: Experiences 255

Chapter 11: Playing With Toys. 256

Supporting Development and Learning. 258

Creating an Environment for Playing With Toys 259
Selecting Materials for Different Ages   260
Including All Children   264
Setting Up and Displaying Materials   265

Caring and Teaching 266
Responding to and Planning for Each Child   269

Sharing Thoughts About the Value of Toys 273

Chapter 12: Imitating and Pretending. 274

Supporting Development and Learning. 276

Creating an Environment for Pretend Play 277
Selecting Materials for Different Ages   277
Setting Up and Displaying Materials   279

Caring and Teaching 280
Responding to and Planning for Each Child   284

Sharing Thoughts About Imitation and Pretend Play. 287

Chapter 13: Enjoying Stories and Books 288

Supporting Development and Learning. 290

Creating an Environment for Enjoying Stories and Books. 291
Selecting Books for Different Ages   291
Setting Up and Displaying Materials   295

Caring and Teaching. 296
Including All Children   300
Responding to and Planning for Each Child   302

Sharing Thoughts About Enjoying Stories and Books 305

Chapter 14: Connecting With Music and Movement 306

Supporting Development and Learning. 308

Creating an Environment for Music and Movement. 309
Selecting and Displaying Materials   309

Caring and Teaching. 311
Responding to and Planning for Each Child   314

Sharing Thoughts About Music and Movement 317

Chapter 15: Creating With Art 318

Supporting Development and Learning. 320

Creating an Environment for Art. 321
Selecting Materials for Different Ages   321
Setting Up and Displaying Materials   326

Caring and Teaching. 328
Inappropriate Art Activities   331
Responding to and Planning for Each Child   332

Sharing Thoughts About Art Experiences 335

Chapter 16: Tasting and Preparing Food 336

Supporting Development and Learning. 338

Creating an Environment for Tasting and Preparing Foods. 339
Selecting Materials for Different Ages   339
Selecting and Displaying Materials   340
Keeping Children Safe and Heathy   341

Caring and Teaching. 342
Responding to and Planning for Each Child   346

Sharing Thoughts About Tasting and Preparing Food 349

Chapter 17: Exploring Sand and Water 350

Supporting Development and Learning 352

Creating an Environment for Sand and Water Play 353
Selecting Materials for Different Ages   354
Setting Up and Displaying Materials   355

Caring and Teaching 356
Responding to and Planning for Each Child   361

Sharing Thoughts About Exploring Sand and Water 363

Chapter 18: Going Outdoors 364

Supporting Development and Learning 366

Creating an Environment for Outdoor Play 367
Keeping Children Safe and Healthy   368
Outdoor Structures   370
Selecting Materials and Experiences for Different Ages   371
Including All Children   374

Caring and Teaching 375
Responding to and Planning for Each Child   379

Sharing Thoughts About Going Outdoors 381

References 382

General Resources 384

Volume 3: Objectives for Development & Learning 1–206

Part A
Routines

Daily routines are one of the most important ways to put research and theory into practice. By responding consistently to children, you meet the basic needs identified by Abraham Maslow, T. Berry Brazelton, and Stanley Greenspan. Their work focused especially on the physical and social–emotional needs that are discussed in the theory and research section of this book. The way you handle routines also enables you to help children build trust and autonomy, as explained by Erik Erikson. Your consistent and responsive care helps children develop secure attachments with the important people in their lives.

Some of your attitudes and personal beliefs may conflict with what you are learning about good early childhood practices. As your program implements *The Creative Curriculum®*, consider these questions with your colleagues and program director:

• How does *The Creative Curriculum®* align with your beliefs and values?

• Do you disagree with any of the practices described in this section? How and why do your practices differ?

• Will you have to adapt your personal values and beliefs to fit curriculum guidelines? What specific adaptations will you have to make?

Each of the chapters on routines includes questions to encourage you to think about your views about a particular routine. Information on safety and health is included because many routines require attention to those concerns. Because partnerships with families enable you to provide consistent care for each child, each chapter ends with a sample letter that invites families to be your partners in making routines rich learning opportunities for children. The letters are also available from www.TeachingStrategies.com/it2-forms. You may use them as they were written or adapt them as necessary for your program.

Hellos and Good-Byes

Supporting Development and Learning 190

**Creating an Environment for
Hellos and Good-Byes** 191

Caring and Teaching 192
Supporting Children and Families During Hellos
and Good-Byes 192
Supporting Children Emotionally
Throughout the Day 194
Responding to What Children Need 195

**Sharing Thoughts About
Hellos and Good-Byes** 199

Hellos and Good-Byes

Matthew (22 months) begins to cry when his mother says good-bye and reassures him that she will return. Mercedes kneels, puts her arm around Matthew, and says, "You are sad because your mommy left." She pauses and gently pats his back. "It's hard to say good-bye. Mommy will be at work, thinking about you. She will be back later. Let's look at our family picture album together." When Mercedes shows the page with photographs of Matthew's family, he smiles and points to his parents, saying, "Mama, Daddy." Mercedes responds, "Yes, that's Matthew's mama, and there's his daddy. They know that you will be here with me until they come to take you home."

Every day begins as families and children say hello to you and good-bye to one another. Every day ends as children reunite with their families and say good-bye to you. Children, their families, and you all experience strong feelings during these times. These times of the day deserve your attention.

Arrivals set the tone for day. A painful farewell is sometimes harder on parents than on children, who often recover quickly once they feel secure in your care. Parents often feel anxious and guilty when their children are crying as they leave. Because every child is different, you have to be flexible and responsive to what each child and family needs from you.

Reunions at the end of the day can be just as emotional for children and families. A child who said good-bye easily or who adjusted well after a painful good-bye may greet her father joyfully or ignore him. She also might have a temper tantrum or begin to cry because she saved her strong feelings for her family, the people she trusts most. The happy response delights her father, but the others might make him feel rejected, sad, or guilty. Departures need your attention as much as arrivals.

Learning to separate is a lifelong process and an important part of growing up. When you help children learn to manage separations from and reunions with their loved ones, they feel understood and gain self-confidence.

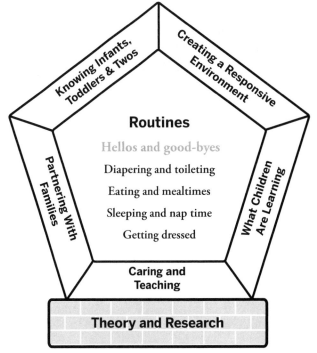

Knowing Infants, Toddlers & Twos

Creating a Responsive Environment

Partnering With Families

What Children Are Learning

Routines

Hellos and good-byes

Diapering and toileting

Eating and mealtimes

Sleeping and nap time

Getting dressed

Caring and Teaching

Theory and Research

Supporting Development and Learning

A child's stage of development influences the way he or she reacts to hellos and good-byes. In part because they involve such strong feelings, hellos and good-byes are opportunities for valuable learning that affects all areas of young children's development.

Learning about themselves and others: As children learn that they can trust you to take care of them and to be their secure base during the day, hellos and good-byes become easier. With your help, children learn to manage the strong feelings evoked by separations and reunions, and, as they develop empathy, they learn to comfort other children. The hello and good-bye rituals that you help young children develop also ease the transitions between home and your program. Family pictures and books connect them to family members who are not immediately present, and they assure children that their families will return at the end of the day.

Learning about moving: Hellos and good-byes provide opportunities for children to develop physical skills. You say, "Wave bye-bye," and model waving for a young infant, who raises her hand to wave good-bye to her mother. You chant, "Peek-a-boo, I see you," as you and the baby cover and uncover your eyes, enjoying this game of disappearing and reappearing. As they make pretend calls to their families, toddlers use their small muscles to push the buttons on toy phones. Twos also practice their fine-motor skills when they scribble a note for a handmade book about saying good-bye.

Learning about the world: Young children show important cognitive development when they understand that, although their families disappear for a while, they return at the end of the day. Pretend play allows them to practice hellos and good-byes with dolls and stuffed animals, and to pretend to talk with their absent families on toy phones.

Learning about communicating: It is no wonder that *bye-bye* is often one of the first words in an infant's vocabulary. Saying good-bye is a frequent experience for a young child. Children continue to develop vocabulary and language—both receptive and expressive—as you label their feelings during separation, reassure them that families will come back, and comfort them by reading stories of babies and mothers who find each other.

Creating an Environment for Hellos and Good-Byes

Special materials in an organized environment make arrivals and departures easier.

Encourage families to bring their child's comfort item from home, such as a special blanket or stuffed animal. Familiar objects help young children feel secure when they are away from those they love. Respect the children's needs and wishes to hold their special objects. Label these items to prevent them from getting lost, and have a place to keep them when children are not using them. Check your safety regulations so that you know when children are old enough to have stuffed animals and untucked blankets in their cribs.

Include pictures of children and their families in your room. Ask families for photographs or take pictures of them with their children. Make an attractive wall display at children's eye level. Consider filling a basket with family pictures so children can carry them around, or make an album or book of family pictures.

Place an interesting toy or material where it can be seen when children arrive. A flowering plant, a photo you took during a neighborhood walk, or a new toy gives parents and children something to explore together as children begin the day. Because arrivals are transitional times, adults and children are sometimes unsure of what to do next. Having something to focus on can be comforting.

Photograph family members in your setting. Take photographs of family members playing and reading with their children. Place the pictures where children can see them easily. These photos show that families are an important part of your program. They are also another way to help children feel connected to their families during the day.

Place toy phones or disconnected real ones near family pictures. Invite children to make pretend calls to their parents. Make pretend calls, yourself, to show them how.

Offer quiet places where toddlers and twos can retreat when they need some quiet time after saying good-bye. Children may choose to go to a special place until they are ready to join the group. These areas can be any quiet places: a comfortable chair, a cozy corner of the room with pillows, or a loft or window seat.

Caring and Teaching

Caring and teaching involves not only managing hellos and good-byes, but also helping children feel connected to their families during the day. The more comfortable children feel in your care, the better they are able to cope with these times of the day.

Your Own Views

- Do you say hello and good-bye to each child and family member every day? What messages do you think your hellos and good-byes (or lack of them) send?

- What do you think about a child who cries a lot when his parents say good-bye? How does his crying make you feel? Do you feel differently about a child who never cries at drop-off time?

- What might explain some parents' attempts to leave without saying good-bye? What are they feeling? How do you feel when parents leave that way? How do the children feel?

- How do you help parents reunite with their children at the end of the day? How does a parent feel when her child cries or keeps playing? How do you feel?

Supporting Children and Families During Hellos and Good-Byes

Hellos and good-byes offer opportunities to build positive, trusting relationships with children and families. Families have different ways of approaching separations and reunions. In some cultures, people believe that very young children should be able to function separately from their families. Other people believe that a mother should never be separated from her infant. As you work with families, try to get to know each family's beliefs and values so that you can support them during hellos and good-byes. Here are some ideas.

Allow sufficient time for hellos and good-byes, to meet individual needs without rushing. For example, a child with a disability may need extra time to adjust. A child learning English as a second language may be comforted by your speaking a few words or singing a simple song in her home language. A child who usually transitions easily may need extra comforting on a particular day.

Spend time with each child and his or her family before the child is left in your care for the first time. As parents get to know you, they will feel more confident about leaving their child in your care. Children will feel more comfortable when they see you interacting positively with their families.

Arrange a transitional period with families. Children need time to get to know you and to feel comfortable in their new setting while a family member is present. Let families know this so they can take the time to ease their child into your program. However, understand that the job situations and other responsibilities of family members may not allow them to stay, even though they would like to do so.

Have families leave something that clearly belongs to them at the program. An object that belongs to a family member is a reminder to the child that his mother or father will be back. The parent might say to the child, "I'm leaving the book I'm reading with you. Will you keep it with your things so we can get it when I pick you up?"

Stay with the child and talk about her feelings if she is upset. When a child has difficulty saying good-bye, it is tempting to rush through the process or to distract the child while a family member leaves. However, doing so might lead the child to distrust you and may make separation even more difficult. You want the child to know that you understand how she feels and that you will help her manage her feelings.

Participate in the rituals that children and families develop. Be available to hold an infant after her mother kisses her on both cheeks and the top of her head. Walk a toddler to the window to wave good-bye and blow kisses. Rituals help children—and adults—feel more secure, because they know what to expect.

Reassure families after a difficult departure. Try to call or e-mail family members during the day to let them know that their child is fine and to explain what you did to comfort the child after they left. This kind of communication is reassuring and builds trust.

Supporting Children Emotionally Throughout the Day

When good-byes are over and children are in your care, they often miss their families and ask about them. An infant might be cranky without an obvious reason. A toddler might ask, "Go home?" only 10 minutes after his father left. There is no reason to ignore or distract children from thinking about their families during the day. In fact, helping children feel connected to their families makes them feel more comfortable in your program. Here are some other things you can do to support children emotionally.

Make daily routines an important part of each day. When children learn that they can depend on consistent routines, it gives them a sense of security that enables them to cope better with separation.

Offer experiences that allow children to express and manage their feelings about hellos and good-byes. Respect children's feelings and provide soothing activities. Music can calm a child's anxiety and make her want to dance. Singing, exploring sand and water, and playing with stuffed animals and dolls are all experiences that help children manage their feelings.

Encourage play that helps children master separating and reuniting. Play games such as peek-a-boo. Offer other opportunities for children to appear and disappear, such as by playing in tunnels, cardboard boxes with doors that open and close, or tents made by draping a blanket over a table. Provide props for toddlers and twos, such as hats, briefcases, cloth bags, and empty food boxes. Encourage them to pretend that they are leaving for work or the store and coming home again. Toddlers and twos also enjoy playing hide-and-seek.

Read books with children about separations and reunions. Books such as *Are You My Mother?* (*¿Eres tu mi mamá?*), by P. D. Eastman, and *The Runaway Bunny,* by Margaret Wise Brown, can help children understand separation and reunion as they hear about the experiences of others. In the first book, a little bird falls from the nest and asks everyone, "Are you my mother?" until he finally finds her. In the second book, a bunny plays an imaginary game of hide-and-seek with his mother. He imagines that he will run away, and she assures him that she will always find him. Also consider writing your own books.

Recognize that children are competent. Children sense when you have confidence in their ability to separate from family members and function well. Your interactions with them help children recognize their own abilities.

Responding to What Children Need

Infants, toddlers, and twos behave differently during hellos and good-byes, depending on their developmental level, temperament, what is happening at home, their physical health, or even the weather.

Young infants who come to your program before they are 6 months old may not have difficulty separating from a family member. During these early months, most babies adjust well to new situations and teachers if their needs are met promptly and consistently. If your care is loving and responsive, very young infants are unlikely to have difficulty during good-byes.

Julio's father is rushed today. He hands Julio (4 months) to Linda quickly, puts the clothes he brought from home on the shelf, kisses Julio's head, and says good-bye. Julio begins to cry, and Linda feels his muscles tense.	
Linda's Thoughts and Questions	Julio is feeling uncomfortable because his morning routine has been rushed. He is learning to communicate his feelings.
	I wonder whether he is reacting to his father's mood.
	How can I comfort him?
How Linda Responds	"My pequeño bebé," Linda says as she rubs Julio's back.
	His crying calms to a soft whimper, and his body begins to relax.
	Linda gets Julio's favorite stuffed animal. "Would you like your soft perrito?"
	Julio reaches for the stuffed dog, holds it, and snuggles up to Linda.
What Julio Might Be Learning	To recognize and reach out to familiar adults (*Objective 2, Establishes and sustains positive relationships; Dimension a, Forms relationships with adults*)
	To express a variety of emotions and needs by using facial expressions, body movements, and vocalizations (*Objective 1, Regulates own emotions and behaviors; Dimension a, Manages feelings*)
	To use his whole hand to grasp objects (*Objective 7, Demonstrates fine-motor strength and coordination; Dimension a, Uses fingers and hands*)

Mobile infants typically show more of a preference than young infants to be with family members and special adults. Around the age of 8–12 months, children often develop anxiety about being separated from the special adults with whom they have bonded. While helping a child through difficult separations may be challenging for both you and the child, remember that the difficulty is a sign that the child has a secure, healthy attachment with his parents. Your job is to build a trusting relationship with him so that he can develop a secure attachment with you as well.

Willard (11 months) returns to child care after a family vacation. Grace greets him warmly, but he clings to his mother. Grace suggests that she stay for a little while. When Grace joins them, Willard looks at his mother, puts his hands on her leg, and looks at Grace. Grace smiles and says, "Hi, Willard. I see that you are looking at me." Willard smiles slightly and turns, burying his face in his mother's arm. When Willard looks at Grace again, he is smiling. Grace says, "Oh, Willard, I missed your smile. I'm so glad you are back!" Willard reaches out and puts his hand on Grace's hand. She gives it noisy kisses. Willard squeals with laughter. His mother gets up to leave. Willard grabs her legs and screams. His mother says, "I'm sorry, Willard, but I have to leave."	
Grace's Thoughts and Questions	Willard has not seen me for a couple of weeks. He wants to stay with his mother, but I know his mother has to leave. How can I comfort him and help him feel safe with me again?
How Grace Responds	Grace gently helps Willard let go of his mother's legs and lifts him into her arms. "It is very hard to say good-bye to Mommy. You are sad to see her go." Willard continues to cry loudly, and he screams as she leaves. Grace rubs his back and continues to talk to him in a soothing voice. "Oh, you love your mommy very much." She walks around with Willard, gently rocking him in her arms. Willard continues to cry and buries his face in Grace's shoulder. Grace gently strokes Willard's head and says, "I'm so glad that I'm getting to hold you right now."
What Willard Might Be Learning	To find security in being with familiar people (*Objective 2, Establishes and sustains positive relationships; Dimension a, Forms relationships with adults*) To use others' facial expressions, gestures, or voices to guide his feelings (*Objective 2, Establishes and sustains positive relationships; Dimension b, Responds to emotional cues*)

Toddlers and twos may cheerfully wave good-bye to their families on some days. On other days, they may cling so tightly to their parents that you have to pull them off gently so that their parents can leave. The same clingy child may ignore a family member who comes to pick her up. If you have established a nurturing relationship with children and if they have a consistent routine, then, even on the most challenging days, children will know that they can trust you to ease them through difficult times.

When his father arrives, Matthew (22 months) is playing happily on the slide. Matthew ignores him and continues playing. Mercedes talks to Matthew's dad about how Matthew has become skilled at going up and down all by himself. Mercedes then walks over to Matthew and says, "Matthew, it is time to go home with your daddy." Matthew shakes his head and says, "No."	
Mercedes' Thoughts and Questions	I don't want Matthew's father to feel badly because Matthew is acting as though he doesn't want to leave. I should explain how hard transitions are. Children need our help to switch from one activity to another. What can I say to help Matthew transition to going home?
How Mercedes Responds	Mercedes says, "Matthew, you're having fun on that slide." Matthew smiles and says, "Slide down." Mercedes explains, "You may go up and down the slide two more times. Then it is time to go home." Matthew goes up and down the slide. Mercedes cheers and says, "One." When he heads up the stairs again, Mercedes says, "Last time, Matthew. Make it a good one!" After Matthew slides down, Mercedes scoops him up and kisses him on the cheek. As they walk to the gate, Mercedes explains to his father the challenge of toddler transitions.
What Matthew Might Be Learning	To follow simple directions and sometimes test limits (*Objective 1, Regulates own emotions and behaviors; Dimension b, Follows limits and expectations*) To balance while moving his arms and legs in active play (*Objective 5, Demonstrates balancing skills*) To understand simple directions and explanations (*Objective 8, Listens to and understands increasingly complex language; Dimension b, Follows directions*) To speak in two-word phrases (*Objective 9, Uses language to express thoughts and needs; Dimension c, Uses conventional grammar*)

Dear Families:

Every day, you and your child say good-bye to one another in the morning and hello again in the afternoon. These hellos and good-byes are children's first steps on a lifelong journey of learning how to separate from and reunite with the important people in their lives. Learning to say hello and good-bye to people we love is a process, not something to be achieved in the first week, month, or even year of child care. Indeed, after many years of experience, we adults sometimes find it difficult to separate and reunite. We give special attention to hellos and good-byes in our program because they are such a major part of your child's life—now and always. Being able to separate is necessary if children are going to develop as confident and capable individuals. Learning to reunite is equally important.

How We Can Work Together

- **Try to spend some time here with your child, when you arrive and before you leave each day.** Your presence will help make the transition between home and child care easier for your child.

- **Never leave without saying good-bye to your child.** It is tempting to leave quietly if your child is busy and not noticing you. By saying good-bye, you strengthen your child's trust in you. Your child knows that you will not disappear without warning. When you are about to leave in the morning, I will be happy to help you and your child say good-bye.

- **Create hello and good-bye rituals.** A good-bye ritual might be as simple as giving your child a giant hug before you leave. A hello might be to come into the room, kneel near your child, smile, open you arms wide, and softly call his name. Having rituals offers both of you the comfort of knowing what to do.

- **Every day is different.** Be aware that, on some days, good-byes and hellos will be harder than on other days. Your child's stage of development and other factors, such as being hungry, tired, or upset by a change in your schedule, can make saying good-bye and hello difficult.

- **Bring familiar items from home.** We welcome family photos and other reminders of home that we may keep where your child can reach them. Seeing these special objects will help your child feel connected to you throughout the day.

By working together, we can help your child feel comfortable, secure, and confident in child care.

Sincerely,

Diapering and Toileting

Supporting Development and Learning 202

**Creating an Environment for
Diapering and Toileting**   203
The Diaper-Changing Station   203
The Toileting Area   204

Caring and Teaching   205
Keeping Children Safe and Healthy   205
Responding to What Children Need   206
Working in Partnership With Families   212

**Sharing Thoughts About
Diapering and Toileting**   213

Diapering and Toileting

Grace explains, "I'm going to change that wet diaper," before gently picking up Willard (11 months). As she places him on the changing table, she invites conversation by saying, "You are wearing bright blue pants today. Did your Daddy put them on you this morning?" Willard says, "Dada." Grace continues, "We're going to put those bright blue pants right back on as soon as we're finished, okay?" As Grace pulls off Willard's pants, he touches his tummy. "That's your tummy," she explains. "Are you giving your tummy a little pat?"

If a child's diaper is changed six times a day until he is 30 months old, he will have had his diaper changed more than 5,400 times. Anything a child experiences 5,400 times is an important part of life for him and for those who create the experience.

Diapering offers a chance to focus all of your attention on a single child. You can talk with each other, sing, or play a game of "Where are your toes?" When you approach diapering as an opportunity for meaningful interactions rather than a task to hurry through, you teach children important lessons: that bodily functions are a normal, healthy part of everyday life and that interactions with others are rewarding.

Between 2 and 3 years of age, children typically become physically, cognitively, and emotionally ready to begin using the toilet. If you and the child's family follow the child's lead, are supportive, work together, and avoid power struggles, you can help make mastering the skill of using the toilet a pleasant learning experience. Their child will also develop the self-confidence that comes with gaining self-control.

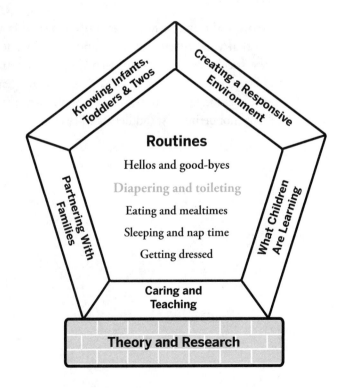

Supporting Development and Learning

Perhaps you have found yourself racing through diaper changes or wishing that all the children you care for had already graduated to underpants. However, diapering and toileting are times for caring and learning, and, as always, what you say and do make a difference in what children learn and how they feel about themselves.

Learning about themselves and others: When young infants begin needing a diaper change at about the same time each day, they have taken an important first step in regulating their own behavior. As 2-year-olds, children continue learning about themselves as they take the giant step of toilet learning. Being able to use the toilet helps 2-year-olds feel good about their bodies, delighted with their new personal care skill, and proud to say, "I flushed! I'm big now!" As 2-year-olds gather in the bathroom, they learn that everybody pees and poops! Children's trust in teachers is built gradually through such care as having wet diapers changed consistently and having toileting accidents handled in a matter-of-fact way.

Learning about moving: As infants, toddlers, and twos develop, they become more active participants in diapering. They practice gross-motor skills as they walk up the steps to the diaper-changing table, and they develop fine-motor skills as they help you take off or put on their pants, snap the snap, and button the large button. Learning to use the toilet requires children to control an important muscle in their body, the sphincter.

Learning about the world: Young children are curious about everything. Diapering and toileting hold many mysteries. How does my body work? Where does the water come from when I turn on the faucet? Why does the toilet make a loud sound when I push the handle? What happens to my poop when I flush? Diapering and toileting help infants, toddlers, and twos learn about how things can be used, and they provide many opportunities to explore cause and effect.

Learning about communicating: Diapering is a time for one-on-one conversations. Infants learn that you are listening and understand what they are communicating when you respond to the special cry that means that they are wet and uncomfortable. Children's vocabularies and language skills grow when you talk about what you are doing as you change their diapers and name body parts and clothing. Books about toileting, such as *Everyone Poops* by Taro Gomi, delight mobile infants, toddlers, and twos.

Creating an Environment for Diapering and Toileting

You and the children will spend lots of time at the diapering table and in the bathroom, so it is important to make the diapering and toileting areas pleasant and attractive. When a space is inviting, you are more likely to relax. The children will sense this and be more relaxed, too. You can add special touches, such as a shatterproof mirror (out of children's reach) or pictures of children.

Remember that convenience is important as well. You will need to have all of your supplies nearby: diapers, wipes, clean clothes, gloves, and bleach solution. Diapering and toileting go smoothly and safely when the area is well-arranged area and has ample room for storage.

The Diaper-Changing Station

Choose the right location. A diaper-changing station should be next to a handwashing sink and away from food preparation areas. This space should be used only for diapering.

Make sure the area is safe and sanitary. Changing surfaces should be nonporous and kept in good repair. They should be surrounded by railings or barriers at least 6 inches high. (Avoid straps. They are easily contaminated and do not keep children safe.) Provide a commercial-grade, step-on, foot-pedaled, or other type of hands-free diaper can. Follow procedures for cleaning and sanitizing the surface after each diaper change.

Make it easy on your back. Most people find that a convenient height for the changing surface is 28–32 inches from the floor. Step-up stairs save you from lifting heavy toddlers and twos. Toddlers often prefer to be changed while they are standing up. Try letting them stand on a mat or use a platform with handholds while you are changing their diapers. Be sure to clean and sanitize the area as you would a changing table.

The Toileting Area

Make it as easy as possible for children to use the toilet independently.
Child-sized toilets and sinks are ideal. If your program does not have child-sized equipment, the American Academy of Pediatrics and the American Public Health Association recommend that you use modified toilet seats and step aids for toilet learning.[28] They discourage using potty chairs because they are difficult to clean and sanitize. If you use potty chairs, be sure to follow the guidance on cleaning and sanitizing them. Arrange the environment so children can be successful and feel competent. If toilets and sinks are not child-height, provide a step stool to help children reach them. Place paper towels within the children's reach, close to the sink. Display photographs of children washing their hands, brushing their teeth, or tossing a paper towel in the trash can.

Adapt the area as necessary for toddlers and twos with disabilities. Many different types of potty seats are designed to meet the needs of children with various disabilities. Families and therapists can advise you about appropriate equipment. If a child uses a wheelchair or walker, be sure to allow enough space in the bathroom. You will also need handrails to make it easy to transfer between the wheelchair and toilet.

Caring and Teaching

Infants, toddlers, and twos can tell how you feel about diapering and toileting by your tone of voice, body tension, and facial expression as they experience these routines with you. Because you are so important to the children in your care, it is important to view diapering and toileting positively.

Your Own Views

- How do you feel when you are changing diapers? How do your feelings about diaper changing influence your interactions with children during this routine?

- How do you feel when a child has a toileting accident? What do you say or do? How does this makes the child feel?

- What do you want to teach children about their bodies while they are learning to use the toilet?

Keeping Children Safe and Healthy

One of your most important responsibilities as a teacher is to keep children safe and healthy. Diapering involves germs that may spread if you are not careful. Stools sometimes carry germs that can cause illnesses with diarrhea and vomiting, as well as serious diseases such as hepatitis A. For this reason, procedures for diaper changing and handwashing must be followed carefully. Follow these guidelines to make diapering and toileting as safe and healthy possible:

Learn your program's policies. For instance, does your program use disposable or cloth diapers? What are your program's policies on the use of gloves or diaper creams? While you must follow universal precautions and wear gloves when blood is present, some programs also recommend or require gloves for routine diapering. If you do use gloves, you have to know when to put them on and how to take them off to avoid contamination.

Follow a recommended procedure for changing diapers. Practice diaper changing until it becomes second nature to you. While you are diapering, remember to talk with the child and take advantage of this time to be together one-on-one.

Schedule regular times to check children's diapers and change diapers between times as needed. The American Academy of Pediatrics and the American Public Health Association recommend that diapers be checked at least hourly for wetness and feces.[29] Following a schedule will enable you to guide other children to activities that do not require your active participation, so you can pay attention to the child whose diaper you are changing.

Have everything you need nearby before you start diapering. This way, you can focus on the child, and you will not have to ask a busy colleague to assist you.

Keep a hand on the child at all times. That is the only way to guarantee the child's safety. Never leave a child alone, even for a moment.

Remain aware of the rest of the group as you change a diaper. Watch, listen, and use your good sense to recognize when you are needed by other children. Try to arrange the diaper-changing table so that you are facing toward, rather than away from, the room. If this is not possible, hang a mirror behind the table so you can watch the rest of the group.

Responding to What Children Need

Depending on their developmental levels and personal characteristics, infants, toddlers, and twos react to diapering and toileting very differently. Your responses will change according to what a child needs from you. All children can learn to use the toilet, except children with medical conditions where the necessary muscles do not function adequately, such as spina bifida. Toilet learning may be a little different for children with disabilities. Talk with each family and encourage them to check with a specialist about the best approach. Ask them to share what they learn so you can work together.

Linda smiles at Julio (4 months) and sings to him while she is changing his diaper. He gazes into her eyes and relaxes.

Young infants interact with you individually during diapering. They also begin exploring and learning about their bodies and things around them. They vocalize back and forth, pausing to listen as you converse together.

Julio (4 months) has been lying on a blanket, smiling at Linda, waving his arms, and kicking his legs. He begins to grimace, whimper, and squirm. Linda smells an odor. "You have a poopy diaper, Julio," she explains. "Let's get you changed right away!" Linda picks him up, takes him to the diaper table, and lays him down. Julio looks at Linda as she chats with him. "Look, you're all clean," she says as she puts on a fresh diaper. She continues talking to him as she gets him dressed and washes his hands.

Linda's Thoughts and Questions	Julio's way of letting me know that he has a wet diaper is to make faces, whimper, and squirm.
	I think he needed to be changed around this time yesterday. I wonder if he's beginning to need a diaper change at the same time every day.
How Linda Responds	Linda changes Julio's diaper as soon as she notices his cues. She talks to Julio, explaining what she is doing. "First we have to take the messy diaper off, and then I will clean your bottom. All clean!" she says, looking back at him as he looks at her. "Time for the dry diaper." After the diaper is on, she washes Julio's hands, smiles, and says, "All done!" Julio smiles back.
What Julio Might Be Learning	To recognize and reach out to familiar adults (*Objective 2, Establishes and sustains positive relationships; Dimension a, Forms relationships with adults*)
	To develop a routine pattern for when he needs his diaper changed (*Objective 1, Regulates own emotions and behaviors; Dimension c, Takes care of own needs appropriately*)
	To show interest in the speech of others (*Objective 8, Listens to and understands increasingly complex language; Dimension a, Comprehends language*)
	To use facial expressions, vocalizations, and body movements to communicate (*Objective 9, Uses language to express thoughts and needs; Dimension a, Uses an expanding expressive vocabulary*)

Mobile infants participate increasingly in the diapering routine. They lift their legs so you can take off the diaper, hold their hands out to be washed, tug on wet pants, and bring you a clean diaper. They begin to learn new words, such as the names of body parts and clothes, and concepts such as up–down, wet–dry, open–close, and cool–warm.

Brooks lifts Abby (14 months) onto the changing table, explaining, "It's time to change your wet diaper, Abby." As soon as Brooks lays her down, Abby quickly rolls over and begins to crawl. Brooks keeps her hand on Abby's back and acknowledges, "Abby, you want to move."	
Brooks' Thoughts and Questions	Abby really enjoys practicing her motor skills. She wants to move, not lie still, but she needs to have her very wet diaper changed. I wonder how to engage her in this routine. How can I acknowledge her desire to move and still change her diaper?
How Brooks Responds	Brooks tells Abby, "I know you want to get down. As soon as I change your diaper, you may get down." "Dow," repeats Abby, recognizing the familiar word. Brooks continues, "Yes, up and down. Abby, now it is time to roll over so that we can change your diaper," She helps Abby roll onto her back and begins to change her diaper, talking to her throughout the process. Abby reaches in the direction of the stack of diapers. "Thank you, Abby. You do need a clean diaper. Will you please hold it for me?" She hands the diaper to Abby.
What Abby Might Be Learning	To begin to be receptive to verbal redirection (*Objective 1, Regulates own emotions and behaviors*; *Dimension b, Follows limits and expectations*) To begin to move from place to place (*Objective 4, Demonstrates traveling skills*) To understand simple multiword speech in familiar contexts (*Objective 8, Listens to and understands increasingly complex language*; Dimension a, *Comprehends language*) To use word-like sounds to communicate (*Objective 9, Uses language to express thoughts and needs*; *Dimension b, Speaks clearly*)

Toddlers are becoming very interested in their bodies and bodily functions. They are able to participate more actively in diapering. They can get their own diapers from their cubbies, pull down their own pants, and often try to take off their wet diapers.

Matthew (22 months) looks at Mercedes, points to his diaper, and says, "Wet." Mercedes reaches for Matthew's hand and says, "Thank you for telling me that you are wet, Matthew. Let's go change your diaper." Matthew shakes his head, clenches his hands into fists, frowns, and insists, "No! Me do!"	
Mercedes' Thoughts and Questions	Lately Matthew has been letting me know when he is wet. However, this is the second time that he has protested when I've thanked him and then tried to change his diaper. He wants to be more involved in the diaper-changing process. How can I give Matthew the opportunity to participate in diaper changing but still follow all of the diapering steps needed to maintain a safe and healthy environment?
How Mercedes Responds	"Matthew, would you like to help me change your diaper?" Matthew nods his head up and down. As Mercedes points to the cubby where his diapers are kept, she asks, "Will you please get a clean diaper for us to use?" Matthew gets a diaper and hands it to her. "Thank you, Matthew. Will you please take your shorts off now?" Matthew pulls at his shorts. It takes him a few tries, but, with some help, he is able to pull them down and step out of them. He smiles at Mercedes and exclaims, "Did it!" As she helps him walk up the steps to the changing table, Mercedes acknowledges, "You took your pants off all by yourself! Okay, let's change that diaper."
What Matthew Might Be Learning	To follow simple directions (*Objective 1, Regulates own emotions and behaviors; Dimension b, Follows limits and expectations*) To try more complex personal care tasks with increasing success (*Objective 1, Regulates own emotions and behaviors; Dimension c, Takes care of own needs appropriately*) To demonstrate understanding of simple directions and questions (*Objective 8, Listens to and understands increasingly complex language; Dimension b, Follows directions*) To speak in two-word phrases (*Objective 9, Uses language to express thoughts and needs; Dimension c, Uses conventional grammar*)

Twos are about to accomplish a special task—toilet learning—and you have an important role to play. Here are some of the ways that children show that they are becoming more aware of their bodily functions and that they will soon be ready for toilet learning:

• staying dry for long periods of time

• wanting to sit on the toilet with their clothes on

• telling you that they are wet, had a bowel movement, or are going to (although usually too late to get them to the bathroom in time)

• saying that they want to use the toilet and talking about their urine and bowel movements, using whatever words are used at home

To help a child learn to use the toilet, follow these steps:

• Watch for the signs that children are ready. Remember that 2-year-olds do not automatically become ready for toilet learning on their second birthday. While some twos show signs of readiness, many children are not ready to undertake this big step until they are at least 30 months old.

• When they seem ready, encourage children to use the toilet. Talk with them consistently and calmly, but without undue pressure or shaming them.

• Frequently remind children to go to the toilet. That way, they might not get so involved in what they are doing that they forget and have an accident. Take advantage of group potty time so children can see and learn from one another.

• Acknowledge children's successes.

• Allow children to see their urine and bowel movements and invite them to help flush them away if they choose.

Expect twos to have toileting accidents as they learn to control when and where they go to the bathroom. If you treat their toileting accidents matter-of-factly, children will develop positive attitudes about using the toilet.

Gena (30 months) is busy building a farm for a new set of animals that Ivan put out this morning. All of a sudden she begins to cry. Ivan walks over and asks "Gena, what happened? I saw you playing with the new animals, and now you're crying." Gena points to her wet pants. "I forgot," she says. Ivan responds, "That's okay. Accidents happen. Let's get you into some dry clothes so you can be comfortable. Then you can finish your farm."	
Ivan's Thoughts and Questions	Gena is beginning to understand that she is expected to use the toilet, and she feels embarrassed when something goes wrong. She sometimes gets so involved in her play that she forgets to use the bathroom. How can I help her remember to go to the bathroom, even while she's absorbed in play?
How Ivan Responds	Ivan helps Gena change into dry clothes and seals her wet ones in a plastic bag for her family to take home and wash. Later in the day, Ivan talks with Gena. He suggests that he help her use the toilet each day after snacks, so she can play without worrying. Gena agrees to the plan.
What Gena Might Be Learning	To understand what behavior is expected, with increasing regularity (*Objective 1, Regulates own emotions and behaviors; Dimension b, Follows limits and expectations*) To continue an activity, despite distractions (*Objective 11, Demonstrates positive approaches to learning; Dimension a, Attends and engages*) To understand increasingly complex and abstract spoken language (*Objective 8, Listens to and understands increasingly complex language; Dimension a, Comprehends language*)

Working in Partnership With Families

Family members and you are likely to have strong feelings about, and perhaps different strategies for, toilet learning. For example, some people think that teaching a child to use the toilet means that the adult should take responsibility for getting the child to the bathroom at the right time. With this in mind, they may begin toilet learning when children are as young as 6 months. Others think that learning to use the toilet should begin when a child is ready to assume responsibility for his or her own use, typically around 30 months of age.

Here are some strategies to help you work with families on diapering and toileting.

Complete the "Individual Care Plan—Family Information Form" when families enter the program. It includes questions about the type of diapers the family uses, how often the child's diaper is changed at home, times that the child usually needs a diaper change, and any special instructions for diapering. (See the Appendix.)

Ask parents whether and how they are helping their child learn to use the toilet at home. Listen carefully and try to understand families' perspectives when they do things differently from you. Ask questions to help you understand their approaches.

Discuss the signs that indicate that a child is ready for toilet learning. Share with families the steps you take to help a child learn to use the toilet. Offer this information at a meeting or workshop for families whose children are starting to use the toilet.

Help families be realistic in their expectations for toilet learning. Remind them that accidents are inevitable and should be treated matter-of-factly. Explain that even children who use the toilet successfully during the day may need to wear diapers at night for a time or may regress temporarily in response to stress. Explain that girls often achieve success sooner because they can more easily control urination. Finally, remind families that each child is different.

Offer resources to families who may be confused or overwhelmed by toilet learning practices. Display books and articles. Encourage family members to share their experiences with each other.

Negotiate differences between families' approaches and yours, if necessary. Things do not have to be done exactly the same at home as in child care, but children need to know what to expect. For example, a child may wear diapers in your program, even though he goes without diapers during weekend days at home. His parents assume responsibility for getting him to the toilet at the right time at home, but you might not be able to do so in your group setting.

Dear Families:

If your child's diaper is changed six times a day for 2 1/2 years, he or she will have had a diaper change more than 5,400 times. Anything experienced 5,400 times is an important part of your child's life—and of yours. Over time, your child will become physically, cognitively, and emotionally ready to begin using the toilet. We will celebrate this milestone together!

While diapering may not be your favorite task, it can be a special time for you and your child. It offers a chance to focus all of your attention on your child. You can talk together, sing, or play a game of "Where are your toes?" When you approach diapering as an opportunity to spend time with your baby, rather than as an unpleasant task to hurry through, you teach your child an important lesson: that bodily functions are a normal, healthy part of everyday life.

How We Can Work Together

- **Let's share information about diapering and toileting.** Tell us how you approach diapering at home. How often do you change your baby's diaper? How do you know that the diaper needs to be changed? Are there any special instructions for diaper changes? Here, we keep track of when we change your child's diapers every day. Be sure to take a look at our daily log and let us know if you have any questions.

- **Please make sure that we have changes of clothing so we can keep your child clean and dry.** Don't be surprised or upset when we send home soiled clothing in a tightly closed plastic bag. Germs can be spread easily during diaper changing, and experts tell us not to rinse soiled clothing at the center. This procedure helps keep your child healthy.

- **Let's talk about approaches to helping children learn to use the toilet.** We'll look together for the signs that your child is ready to learn to use the toilet. We'll also talk regularly about your child's progress. Then we can then decide together about ways to support your child and resolve any differences we may have.

- **Remember that toileting accidents are normal.** Learning to use the toilet takes time. Even children who can use the toilet successfully sometimes have toileting accidents. Having realistic expectations allows us to respond to toileting accidents matter-of-factly. We have some great books that you can read to your child about going to the toilet. *Everyone Poops*, by Taro Gomi, is sure to become a family favorite!

By keeping a sense of perspective and a sense of humor, we can give your child the time and support needed to learn to use the toilet.

Sincerely,

8

Eating and Mealtimes

Supporting Development and Learning 216

Creating an Environment for Eating and Mealtimes 217

Caring and Teaching 218
Keeping Children Safe and Healthy 220
Responding to What Children Need 221
Working in Partnership With Families 226

Sharing Thoughts About Eating and Mealtimes 227

Eating and Mealtimes

Valisha (33 months) has just finished washing her hands. LaToya, who is getting ready for lunch, says, "Valisha, I need some help. Will you please carry these spoons to the table? We need them to eat our lunch." Valisha takes four spoons from LaToya, places one on each placemat, and exclaims, "I did it!" "Thank you," responds LaToya. "What else do we need?" "Napkins," answers Valisha, getting them from the lunch cart. She sits on one of the chairs and distributes the napkins, admitting, "I'm tired." LaToya smiles. "You've been a big help, Valisha. Today we're having one of your favorite lunches: rice and beans." Valisha responds, "Yea! Mommy makes that."

Mealtimes and related activities, such as setting the table, washing hands, talking with others at the table, and brushing teeth, are all learning opportunities. During these activities, you interact with children and help them get to know one another. Through your involvement, they also develop good nutrition and health habits. During mealtimes, infants, toddlers, and twos explore the tastes, colors, textures, and aromas of foods and enjoy a sense of caring and community.

When Linda cradles Julio (4 months) in her arms to give him his bottle, she gives him the message, "You can trust me to take good care of you." When Brooks puts a spoon and a dish of mashed sweet potato on (14-month-old) Abby's plate, her actions say, "Go ahead. Here's a chance to practice feeding yourself." LaToya teaches concepts and social skills when she talks with children about the fact that the green beans are the same color as the playdough they made, reminds them to use the chairs for sitting, and helps them brush their teeth. She also supports their development of healthy habits.

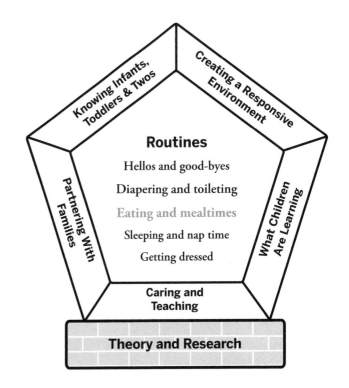

Routines

Hellos and good-byes

Diapering and toileting

Eating and mealtimes

Sleeping and nap time

Getting dressed

Knowing Infants, Toddlers & Twos

Creating a Responsive Environment

Partnering With Families

What Children Are Learning

Caring and Teaching

Theory and Research

Supporting Development and Learning

Here are some of the many things children learn during eating and mealtimes.

Learning about themselves and others: When a mobile infant somewhat successfully guides a spoonful of applesauce to his mouth, his expression suggests his pleasure in feeding himself. As infants learn to regulate their behavior, they develop routine patterns for eating. By the time they are toddlers, they participate in group routines, such as family-style dining. Toddlers not only develop food preferences, but they discover their friends' likes and dislikes, too. Eating and mealtimes are filled with opportunities for infants, toddlers, and twos to develop a range of personal care skills. Invite twos to join in when it is time to clean up after meals and snacks.

Learning about moving: As they use their fingers and spoons to bring food to their mouths, children practice fine-motor skills and refine their eye-hand coordination. Imagine a young infant who curls his fingers around your hand as you give him his bottle. Soon he will use a pincer grasp to pick up the tiny Cheerios® on his plate. Drinking from a cup, beginning to serve food, pouring milk from a very small pitcher, and cleaning up the inevitable spills are some of the everyday activities that promote children's small-muscle development and coordination.

Learning about the world: During mealtimes, infants, toddlers, and twos continue to learn how things work. Children use all five senses to see, smell, taste, touch, and listen to the foods, related objects, and people involved in mealtime experiences. Young infants learn about cause and effect as they tip their bottles when the level of milk drops. Mobile infants solve the problem of how to eat noodles with their fingers. Twos smell lunch being made in the kitchen and say, "Time to eat." Mealtimes also present opportunities for twos to develop mathematical concepts such as *more* and *less*. They also develop spatial awareness when they do such things as pour drinks and spoon food onto their plates from the serving bowl.

Learning about communicating: Mealtime conversations are opportunities for children to hear and practice using interesting, descriptive language as they munch on *crunchy green lettuce* or taste *smooth* infant *cereal*. As mobile infants, toddlers, and twos sit together during mealtimes, they begin to engage in nonverbal and verbal conversations with you and their friends. Toddlers and twos certainly use their expanding language skills to let you know their food preferences.

Creating an Environment for Eating and Mealtimes

Bottles, breast milk, formula, baby food jars, dishes, and spoons are all necessary supplies in an infant classroom. The environment for eating and mealtimes therefore includes places to prepare and store food and to ensure safe food handling. In addition, you need comfortable places to hold and feed young infants, and inviting spaces where small groups of mobile infants, toddlers, and twos can eat together.

Here are some important considerations.

Observe health and safety guidelines when organizing the food-preparation and eating areas. Locate areas for eating and mealtimes away from diapering, toileting, and laundry areas. An infant room must have a handwashing sink and, ideally, a small refrigerator.

Arrange adequate storage and space for food preparation. Storage cabinets, often mounted on the wall, and a counter for food preparation help make this area functional. You also need a place to warm bottles. Some programs warm bottles under hot running water, while others use a bottle warmer or crock pot. It is not safe to warm bottles or baby food jars in a microwave oven because the contents do not heat evenly. Always make sure that electrical cords are safely out of children's reach.

Have comfortable seating for feeding young infants. Because you will be holding young infants in your arms when feeding them, have a comfortable glider or soft chair to sit in. Locate these throughout the room. You do not need to dedicate a space only to feeding young infants.

Provide a comfortable chair and a private space for mothers who are breast-feeding. Include a pillow to support her baby on her lap, a foot rest, and a glass of water to drink.

Have appropriately sized tables and chairs. Once they can support themselves, mobile infants can sit in sturdy infant chairs at low tables. Slightly higher tables and chairs are made for toddlers and twos. Children should sit with their feet touching the floor, rather than in high chairs or at tables with bucket seats, where their legs dangle in the air.

Arrange an eating area for mobile infants, toddlers, and twos. Think about how to arrange your tables to make mealtimes manageable. This will depend partly on the number of tables you need. Most likely no more than 3–4 mobile infants and toddlers will be eating at a time. In a class for 2-year-olds, the group will eat together, with four or five children sitting at tables with a teacher.

Use plates and eating utensils that are unbreakable, safe, and easy to handle. Toddlers can learn to serve themselves by using small plastic pitchers for pouring water, juice, or milk and by using plastic serving bowls. When pitchers and glasses are clear, children can see how much they have poured. Never use Styrofoam™ materials or plastic utensils that can be broken easily. Special utensils, deep-sided bowls, and mugs with two handles make it easier for children to feed themselves.

Make cleanup as easy as possible. Locate your eating space in an area with an easy-to-clean floor, have the children wear bibs, place extra napkins and paper towels nearby, and invite children to help clean up spills.

Caring and Teaching

Being with you is an important part of children's mealtime experiences. Model good manners and the pleasures of social interaction. For young infants, who need to be fed on demand and held when you give them a bottle, mealtime is important one-on-one time with you. Mobile infants are also fed according to individual eating schedules.

For a group of toddlers, of twos, or of mixed ages, family-style dining is a good way to organize mealtimes. In this arrangement, everyone sits together around the table—on low chairs or on your lap, depending on children's ages—so they can see and interact with each other. Toddlers and twos serve themselves, with your help. Children may begin eating as soon as they have food on their plates. Although some families expect children to wait until everyone is served, waiting is difficult for hungry toddlers and twos.

During eating and mealtimes, you build positive relationships with young children while you nurture their bodies. Infants are more comfortable when they are fed by their primary teacher as much as possible. Toddlers and twos also like to sit and eat with their primary teacher. Good experiences at mealtimes help children develop positive attitudes toward food and nutrition.

Your Own Views

- Would you describe yourself as a healthy eater or as someone who does not get proper nutrition? How does your approach to nutrition influence how and what you teach children about healthy eating?

- What should mealtime be like for infants, toddlers, and twos? Should talking be encouraged and, if so, who should talk? Should children be moving around or sitting down? Must children eat everything on their own plates? Should children drink while they eat or after they eat? Should everyone eat together or on their own?

- Have you ever used food as a reward, such as giving a child a cupcake for sitting still at lunch? Have you used it as a punishment, such as not allowing a child to have a snack because he did not put his toys away? If so, what do you think that experience taught the child about food and eating?

Here are some strategies to use during eating and mealtimes.

Feed children when they are hungry. Watch and listen for cues that babies are hungry, and feed them as soon as possible. Before becoming so hungry that they cry, infants often show that they are ready to be fed by opening their mouths, making sucking sounds, and moving their hands randomly. Keep waiting times for mobile infants and toddlers as brief as possible, too. Have the food ready when the children come to the table. Be sure to have everything you need, including food, beverages, dishes, and spoons. You do not want to leave the table to look for missing items.

Always hold young infants when feeding them bottles. Sit in a comfortable chair and snuggle with the baby. Enjoy having infants curl their fingers around yours, helping you hold their bottles. Even when they can hold the bottle by themselves, they still want to be held, enjoying your special time together.

Create a calm and pleasant atmosphere. Transitions that help set a relaxed tone include reading a book together or doing another quiet activity. Allow enough time for a leisurely meal.

Encourage relaxed, friendly conversation. Talk together during mealtimes about familiar topics of interest to the children, such as the tastes and smells of the foods you are eating, activities you did earlier in the day, and plans for the afternoon. Encourage children to let you know what they want and need during mealtimes.

Create an after-meal ritual with mobile infants and with toddlers and twos. For example, encourage children to stay at the table and talk with each other until everyone has finished. Be sure, however, to permit children who cannot wait to leave the table to brush their teeth or work on a puzzle until everyone has finished eating.

Avoid struggling over food. Encourage children to try new foods, but do not force them to eat something they do not want. Talk about new foods, serve them in attractive ways, and taste everything yourself. Sometimes toddlers eat just one or two foods for a period of time. If they are given nutritious choices, they get the nutrients they need over the course of a week or a month, even if not at each meal. Allow children to control the quantity of food they eat, do not expect them to eat everything on their plates, and remember to offer choices to toddlers and twos. Never use food as a reward or punishment.

Promote children's growing independence during snack and mealtimes. Encourage children to participate in whatever ways are appropriate for their level of development. Seat an infant on your lap so he can hear and watch the other children. Offer a mobile infant a chance to use her fingers to feed herself. Provide spoons that are easy to hold for toddlers who want to feed themselves. Invite 2-year-olds to help you set the table and do other mealtime tasks.

Offer experiences that encourage children to practice mealtime skills throughout the day. For example, include plates and eating utensils in the pretend play area so children can enact mealtime events. Provide small pitchers and cups for water play. Children can use these to practice pouring liquids. See chapter 15, "Tasting and Preparing Foods", for ideas about involving children in cooking experiences.

Recognize children's new skills and accomplishments. Make a positive comment when you see a child just learning to hold a bottle, drink from a cup, or spread cottage cheese on a cracker. Acknowledging their competence encourages them to practice their skills and attempt new ones.

Consult with specialists about a child with a disability that affects eating. They can advise you about feeding procedures, as well as about appropriate adaptive equipment.

Invite families to join their children for snacks and meals whenever they can. With their help, each child can be given more attention. Having family members present can also ease separation difficulties and help children enjoy eating at the program as much as they enjoy it at home.

Consider the best time for you to eat. Although you want to be a good model for children, you may find that trying to eat at the same time you are supervising a group at the table is too much. You may prefer to have your lunch during a more quiet time. In some programs, teachers eat a small portion of their lunch with the children and the rest of their meal during their lunch break.

Keeping Children Safe and Healthy

Here are some health and safety points to consider and share with families, whether you or the families provide food for the children.

Learn the rules for handling food safely. Carefully follow the instructions for mixing formula, storing breast milk, serving semisolid and solid baby food safely, and so forth. Clean and sanitize food preparation and eating areas with a surface bleach solution. Your local food service inspector or sanitarian can help you learn how to handle food to minimize the risk of food-borne illnesses.

Promote good health and safety practices. Handwashing is extremely important when preparing foods, and before and after eating. Wash your hands, wash infants' hands, and help toddlers and twos wash their hands. Wipe infants' teeth with a soft cloth, and help older children with toothbrushing. Do not allow children to eat when walking, running, playing, lying down, or riding in vehicles. Store cleaning materials in locked cabinets, out of the reach of children. Do not use microwave ovens to heat bottles or baby food jars.

Learn about good nutrition for infants, toddlers, and twos. The United States Department of Agriculture (USDA) Child and Adult Care Food Program (CACFP) provides guidelines for nutritious meals and snacks for children birth to age 3. The Food and Nutrition Service publishes *Feeding Infants: A Guide for Use in the Child Nutrition Program*, which can be downloaded from the USDA Web site. Model good nutrition practices for children.

Be aware of and follow food safety precautions. For example, do not give honey to infants under 12 months of age because it may carry harmful bacteria. Before they are 12 months old, avoid giving infants white table sugar, artificial sweeteners, corn syrup, egg whites, fried foods, shellfish, raw onions, and processed meats. Do not offer tomatoes and pineapple to infants who are younger than 1 year. The high acidity of these foods can harm delicate mouth tissues.

Avoid serving foods that may cause choking. Children under 3 years should not eat certain foods because they are choking hazards. Hot dogs and peanuts are the most frequent causes of choking in children under age three. Other foods that can cause a young child to choke include raw carrots; raisins and similar dried fruit, such as cherries or cranberries; popcorn; whole grapes; blueberries; whole olives; corn; uncooked peas; nuts; peanut butter; crumbly cookies or crackers; jelly beans; and hard candy.

Never prop bottles. Putting a baby to bed with a bottle of milk or juice can cause ear infections, choking, and bottlemouth, a severe form of tooth decay that may cause tooth loss.

Be aware of children's allergies. Ask each family whether their child has allergies to any foods. If so, post that information where everyone working with the child will see it. Be prepared to handle an allergic reaction. Find out what symptoms to watch for and what you need to do if the child has an adverse reaction. Common food allergies include chocolate, strawberries, peanut butter, other nuts, and tofu.

Stop to burp young infants. Stop every 3–5 minutes or when a child has consumed 2–3 ounces of formula or milk. This rest lets the child slow down and prevents her from swallowing too much air. If the child does not burp, place her in an upright position for 15 minutes after the feeding to prevent spitting up. Ask the family what burping technique their baby prefers. For example, you might hold the baby upright on your shoulder and gently pat her back, or sit the baby on your lap and pat her back while supporting her head and neck. Another technique is to rest the baby over your lap, tummy down; lift and support his head so it is higher than his chest; and pat his back.

Work with families to comfort babies with colic. About 10–20 percent of young infants in Western cultures develop colic, a condition that can last through the fourth month. Babies with colic tend to cry loudly, uncontrollably, and for a long time; extend or pull their legs up to their stomachs; have enlarged stomachs; and/or pass gas. There is often no apparent cause for colic, but most children outgrow the condition.

Responding to What Children Need

Babies' mouth patterns and hand and body skills affect the kinds of foods they are able to eat, as well as how they should be fed. Here is general information about what infants, toddlers, and twos are able to do, the kinds of food they can eat, and how to feed them.

Young infants are born with nursing reflexes. A baby turns his head toward an object, such as a nipple, when his mouth, lip, cheek, or chin is touched. When a baby's lips are touched, his tongue moves out of his mouth. This reflex allows feeding from the breast or bottle but not from a spoon or cup. Feeding solid foods is not recommended until a baby is 4–6 months old.

Between about 4 and 7 months of age, babies develop new skills that enable them to eat semisolid foods, such as infant cereal with iron and strained vegetables and fruit. They open their mouths when they see food. They can now move their tongues up and down, and swallow many foods without choking. They can sit with support, have good head control, and use their whole hands to grasp objects. Infants who are eating soft or solid foods but who are not yet able to sit alone should sit in your lap while you feed them. Place the food on a nearby table or counter.

Janet feeds Jasmine (8 months) some applesauce while sitting at a child-size table. As Jasmine opens her mouth, Janet uses the spoon to direct applesauce into it. Janet comments, "I know you like applesauce, Jasmine, because you always finish the bowlful." As Janet feeds her, Jasmine dips her right hand into the bowl, looks up at Janet, and pops her hand into her mouth. Most of the applesauce falls out of Jasmine's hand before it reaches her mouth.

Janet's Thoughts and Questions	Jasmine really wants to feed herself, although she does not always get the food into her mouth.
	It would be so much easier for me to feed her, but I know that it's important to encourage her desire to feed herself and to support her developing self-feeding skills.
	If I let Jasmine feed herself, will she get enough to eat?
How Janet Responds	As Janet wipes up the spilled applesauce, she comments, "It's great that you're feeding yourself, Jasmine. Applesauce is very slippery."
	"Jasmine, I want to be sure you eat enough food. Let's do this: I'll feed you one spoonful of applesauce; then you take a turn feeding applesauce to yourself."
What Jasmine Might Be Learning	To attempt simple personal care tasks (*Objective 1, Regulates own emotions and behaviors*; *Dimension c, Takes care of own needs appropriately*)
	To use her whole hand to grasp and drop objects (*Objective 7, Demonstrates fine-motor strength and coordination*; *Dimension a, Uses fingers and hands*
	To notice particular characteristics of objects (*Objective 26, Demonstrates knowledge of the physical properties of objects and materials*)
	To demonstrate awareness of a problem (*Objective 11, Demonstrates positive approaches to learning*; *Dimension c, Solves problems*)

Mobile infants, from about 8–11 months, learn to move their tongues from side to side. They have some teeth and begin to chew. They use their thumb and index finger to pick up objects, learn to eat from a spoon, drink milk from a cup with less spilling, and begin to feed themselves with their hands. Now they are ready to eat mashed, diced or strained fruit, vegetables, meat, poultry, beans, and peas. They can also eat cottage cheese, yogurt, cheese strips, pieces of soft bread, and crackers. They continue to drink breast milk or iron-fortified formula and can also drink fruit juice, but now they drink from a cup as well as a bottle. At about 11 months, they begin to hold a cup and, with help, begin spoon-feeding themselves. Once infants can sit comfortably, they can sit in low, sturdy infant chairs at low tables.

Barbara is sitting with Leo (18 months) and two other children at a low table as they eat lunch. She says, "M-m-m. These crackers are nice and crunchy." Suddenly, Leo reaches over and grabs two crackers from Wanda's plate. He starts to eat one of the crackers but stops when Wanda starts to scream. Leo quickly puts the crackers back on Wanda's plate.	
Barbara's Thoughts and Questions	Wow! Leo actually put the crackers back on Wanda's plate when she protested. I've been trying to help him use other children's reactions to guide his behavior. Maybe it's beginning to work!
How Barbara Responds	"Leo, Wanda was angry when you took her crackers. She's glad you put them back. Would you like some more crackers?" Leo nods his head up and down. As she moves the plate closer to him, Barbara explains, "You may take some from this big plate."
What Leo Might Be Learning	To use other's facial expressions, gestures, or voices to guide his own behavior; to respond to the emotions of others (*Objective 2, Establishes and sustains positive relationships; Dimension b, Responds to emotional cues*)

To participate in group routines (*Objective 2, Establishes and sustains positive relationships; Dimension c, Interacts with peers*) |

Toddlers and twos continue to refine their fine-motor skills and eye-hand coordination. This enables them to participate even more in feeding themselves. They learn to hold and drink from a cup, eat with a spoon, and later eat with a fork. They begin serving themselves from bowls and even pour milk from a very small pitcher.

The physical growth of toddlers slows, so their appetites often decrease. As they become more successful at regulating their behavior, they usually stop eating when they are full. They need small servings of food throughout the day. Toddlers and twos often have strong food likes and dislikes, eat one favorite food for a while, and then often refuse to eat the food they used to prefer.

Start family-style meals, with small groups of children sitting at low tables. Provide utensils so they can serve themselves and eat independently. Encourage children to try new foods, but do not force them. They are more likely to try them if you serve foods in an appealing manner. Offer choices and be patient; they may need many opportunities to try a food before they actually eat it.

Valisha (33 months) and Jonisha (33 months) have just finished eating lunch, served family style. Jonisha says, "I want more milk. I can pour it." Then she exclaims, "Oops!" as the milk she is pouring from a small pitcher makes a puddle on the floor. She stands up, goes to the sink, and gets a paper towel. After she tries wiping the spill with the towel, she says, "There's too much. I'll get the mop." She puts the paper towel in the trash can, gets the child-size mop, and, with some help from LaToya, cleans up the spill.	
LaToya's Thoughts and Questions	Jonisha thought of a good solution to the problem of spilled milk. When it didn't work, she thought of and carried out another, more effective solution. I think I can find ways to help her practice pouring at the water table and in the pretend play area. I wonder if that pitcher is just too big for the children.
How LaToya Responds	"Milk sometimes spills, Jonisha. You figured out the best way to clean it up. I think that pitcher might be too big. I'll look for a smaller one, to make it easier to pour milk without spilling it."
What Jonisha Might Be Learning	To use eye–hand coordination while doing increasingly complex tasks (*Objective 7, Demonstrates fine-motor strength and coordination; Dimension a, Uses fingers and hands*) To continue an activity until her goal is reached (*Objective 11, Demonstrates positive approaches to learning; Dimension a, Attends and engages*) To carry out her own plan for solving simple problems (*Objective 11, Demonstrates positive approaches to learning; Dimension c, Solves problems*) To use simple sentences with three or more words (*Objective 9, Uses language to express thoughts and needs; Dimension c, Uses conventional grammar*)

Working in Partnership With Families

The essential role that food plays in family life is influenced by many cultural and family traditions. Eating and mealtimes therefore offer opportunities to strengthen your partnerships with families. Communication with families is necessary to creating familiar mealtimes that are pleasant for children. It is especially important with very young children, because food and feeding practices have to be carefully coordinated between families and the program for health reasons.

For children younger than 3 years, special feeding issues must be discussed with families, preferably at the very beginning of your relationship. These may include nursing, weaning, introducing solid foods, allergies, and, if families provide meals, what food to bring.

Talk with each family about what their child eats at home and in your program. The "Individual Care Plan—Family Information Form" includes questions to guide your conversations with families and to collect specific information about feeding and eating practices at home. Update the form regularly so that you can coordinate closely with the family. When appropriate, discuss the family's plans for introducing solid foods and for weaning. With the knowledge and approval of the child's family, introduce new foods gradually, letting the child try each after the family has first introduced it at home. When you introduce a new food, allow time—usually five days—before introducing another. You need to be sure that the child is not allergic to each new food.

Respect and follow families' preferences and special food requests as much as possible, whether for reasons of health, culture, religion, or personal preference. For example, do not give extra bottles to an infant whose mother wants to continue nursing. If differences arise, discuss them with the family. Be aware that families' viewpoints might be different from yours with regard to such things as self-feeding, messiness at mealtimes, playing with food, and sitting at the table.

Invite mothers to come to the program and nurse their infants at any time. Provide a comfortable place where they can be with their babies without interruption.

Ask families about foods their children eat at home. Share your program's menus. If families provide their children's lunches, suggest safe and nutritious foods. Keep records of what and how much children eat during the day. Give families brief notes with this information, to help them plan their children's meals and snacks at home.

Working with families helps build continuity between home and your program, and it helps children feel comfortable and secure. The following letter to families is another way to communicate about eating and mealtimes.

Dear Families:

Imagine your child eating a meal or snack in child care. What is he or she experiencing? Certainly your child is getting the foods he or she needs to be healthy and strong. Children also experience much more. Snacks and meals—and, for older children, related activities such as setting the table, cleaning up, and brushing their teeth after eating—give your child a chance to feel cared for and to develop personal care, communication, and social skills. Mealtimes also give children chances to begin practicing good nutrition and health habits.

Children's experiences and the attitudes they form now will affect their future eating habits. By modeling healthy practices and making eating a pleasurable and social time, we can lay the groundwork together for nutritious and enjoyable eating for the rest of their lives.

How We Can Work Together

- **Join us for a snack or meal whenever you can.** Your child will love having you with us. So will we! In addition, you will have a chance to see how we do things, and you may ask questions and make suggestions. Of course, if you are nursing your child, please come anytime. We have set up a comfortable place where you can feed your baby without interruption.

- **Let's communicate about changes in your child's diet or eating habits.** For example, please let us know when your pediatrician recommends adding new foods. After you introduce a new food at home, we'll introduce it here at the center. We can also work together when your child is ready to be weaned from the bottle.

- **Give us any information we need to keep your child healthy.** For example, let us know whether your child has allergies or a tendency to gag or choke. Keep us informed of any changes.

- **Please tell us what your child experiences during mealtimes at home.** What does your child eat and drink? What are your child's favorite foods? Do you have special family foods? What do you talk about? How does your child participate? This information will help us give your child a sense of continuity. It enables us to talk about family meals and serve some of the same foods.

- **Please ask us for menus and ideas for mealtimes.** Sometimes it's hard to come up with ideas for lunches. We'll be glad to give you some tips. We welcome your ideas as well.

Together, we can make mealtimes an enjoyable and valuable learning experience for your child.

Sincerely,

Sleeping and Nap Time

Supporting Development and Learning 230

Creating an Environment for Sleeping and Nap Time 231

Caring and Teaching 234
Responding to What Children Need 237
Working in Partnership With Families 240

Sharing Thoughts About Sleeping and Nap Time 241

Sleeping and Nap Time

Leo (18 months) is lying on the cushion in the book nook, rubbing his eyes. Barbara remarks, "You're a sleepy boy, even though your mama said that you slept well last night. You usually don't nap until 11:00, but I think you need an early nap today. Would you like to sit in the rocking chair with me before you lie down?" Leo nods, "Yes." He snuggles on Barbara's lap in the chair. Barbara holds Leo and rocks him until he is ready to lie down on his cot.

Sleep is necessary for healthy growth and development, so sleeping and nap time are important parts of a program for young children. Very young infants sleep most of the day, waking only for diapering, feeding, and other care. Active toddlers and 2-year-olds, by contrast, spend more time awake than asleep, napping for an hour or more to restore their energy. Even a child who does not seem to want to sleep will benefit from a rest time away from group activities. A well-rested child is better able to participate fully in the program.

Because each infant's sleep-wake cycle is likely to be different, meeting the individual needs of the infants in your care can be challenging. Even though toddlers and twos generally sleep on regular schedules and might nap as a group, it is still necessary to look for cues to their individual and changing needs. One child may need to nap earlier than usual on a particular day. Another may sleep for less or more time than he does ordinarily.

Strengthening your relationship with children is as important as meeting their physical needs when you put them to sleep. When you sing a soft lullaby and rock an infant, or read a story and rub a toddler's back at nap time, you show that you care about her well-being and security.

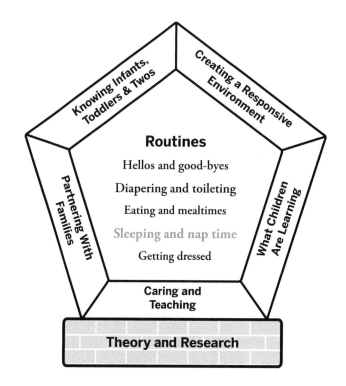

Supporting Development and Learning

Sleeping and nap times are necessary to children's physical, cognitive, and language development, and for their social well-being.

Learning about themselves and others: When infants develop regular sleeping patterns and comfort themselves as they fall asleep, they are showing early signs of regulating their behavior and managing their feelings. Toddlers and twos develop personal care skills as they learn to spread their blankets on their cots and take their shoes off before napping.

Learning about moving: Infants practice large-muscle skills when they roll over in their cribs or pull themselves up to show you that they are awake. Toddlers and twos also practice large-muscle skills as they walk (or toddle) to their cots or mats, carry their favorite books with them, and sit and lie down on their cots. They also learn that it is important to stop moving and rest during the day. Well-rested children have the energy to move their bodies when they are awake, to explore their environment, and to play.

Learning about the world: Infants, toddlers, and twos begin to develop a beginning sense of time and sequence as sleeping and naps conform to a routine. They learn cause and effect and problem solving when their teacher responds to crying, eye rubbing, crankiness, or slowed activity by saying, "You're sleepy. It's time for you to take a nap." They learn how objects function as they use cribs, cots, sheets, and blankets.

Learning about communicating: Children communicate their sleeping needs both nonverbally and verbally. When infants rub their eyes, turn their heads away, and make their cries of fatigue, they signal their need for sleep. When you respond, they learn that their signals are effective. When you explain what you are doing as you put infants, toddlers, and twos in their cribs or help them onto their cots, you are helping them learn language. When you read the delightful rhymes in Mem Fox's *Time for Bed* or other bedtime stories, or sing a favorite lullaby, you are not only helping a child fall asleep, you are also introducing children to the joys of storytelling, the sounds of language, and the rhythm and pitch of music.

Creating an Environment for Sleeping and Nap Time

By themselves, cribs take up a lot of room in an infant environment. In addition, best practice in health care recommends that cribs be three feet apart. Check with your state and local policies to make sure you know what is required in your area. Finding the best arrangement for cribs so that children can sleep and also have a large enough area to play is a challenge. Because each infant sleeps on a personal schedule, you need to create an environment that is conducive to both sleeping and playing.

Some programs solve the problem by having a separate space dedicated just to sleeping. In fact, some state licensing regulations require this arrangement. The American Academy of Pediatrics and the American Public Health Association recommend that separate sleeping rooms for infants have at least 30 square feet per child.[30] In addition, if the room is walled off, a teacher needs to stay with even one child.

By choice or because space is limited, other programs place infants' cribs throughout the room or set them in a bedroom-like area. Where cribs are in the room, low walls or partial wall dividers may be used to reduce some of the surrounding visual stimulation and sounds that interfere with sleeping.

As infants grow, they begin to sleep on a more predictable schedule. Eventually, the individual schedules of the infants in your room will merge. Toddlers and twos generally sleep at the same time. At a regularly scheduled period, place cots throughout the room. Also remember to have a cot available for toddlers and twos who are sleepy when they arrive in the morning or who need to nap earlier than the group.

When setting up a sleeping area for infants and napping spaces for toddlers and twos, these strategies are very important.

Place nap time supplies close to cribs. The less you move around, the more easily children will fall asleep. A comfortable glider chair lets you rock a sleepy baby and then put him in his crib easily.

Have an individual crib, cot, or mat for each child. Assigning cribs, cots, mats, and bedding helps minimize the spread of head lice and infectious diseases. Labeling cribs, cots, and linens with children's names helps reserve their use for individual children.

Make sure cribs are safe. The National Institute of Child Health and Human Development makes these recommendations to reduce the risk of Sudden Infant Death Syndrome (SIDS):[31]

- Use firm crib mattresses.

- Place babies on their backs to sleep.

- Keep pillows, heavy blankets, comforters, and toys out of cribs.

- If a thin blanket is used, make sure it does not reach higher than the baby's chest and that the ends of the blanket are tucked under the crib mattress.

- Make sure babies' heads and faces are uncovered while they sleep.

- Avoid the use of bumper pads, which can block the flow of fresh air and make carbon dioxide build up.

- Watch for strangulation hazards. Make sure that there are no dangling cords from blinds or drapes near cribs.

- Keep side rails up when children are in their cribs. Lower the crib height of the mattress when children begin to sit or stand. Watch for signs that infants have outgrown their cribs, for instance, when they can pull themselves off the crib floor by holding onto the railings. When cribs are no longer safe, move children to cots.

Provide children with clean sheets and bedding. Wash linens whenever they are soiled or wet. Generally, you should wash or send linens home for washing at least weekly. You may need to have linens for infants, toddlers, and twos washed more frequently. Store bedding so that it does not touch the surface of another child's cot. Your local health department can help you learn how to store bedding to help prevent the spread of disease.

Provide evacuation cribs. Having evacuation cribs is an emergency measure. They are special cribs with 4-inch wheels, capable of holding up to five infants. Place an evacuation crib near an emergency exit.

Be sure that each child sleeps in the same place each day. Place cribs, cots, or mats in the same place each day. The regularity eliminates confusion, helps children develop a sense of their own place, and promotes security and trust.

Create peaceful spaces where children can sleep. Absorb noise by using carpeting. Putting curtains on the windows reduces unwanted light. Where lighting is necessary, make it soft. If room barriers are not available, you can move cribs, cots, or mats to places in your room where you can diminish noise and visual stimulation.

Remove all toys, crib gyms, and mobiles from cribs. That helps children understand that cribs are for sleeping, not playing. It also reduces safety concerns.

Provide a place for mothers who are breast-feeding. The sleeping area is generally quiet and private. Many programs allocate a separate section in the area for breast-feeding.

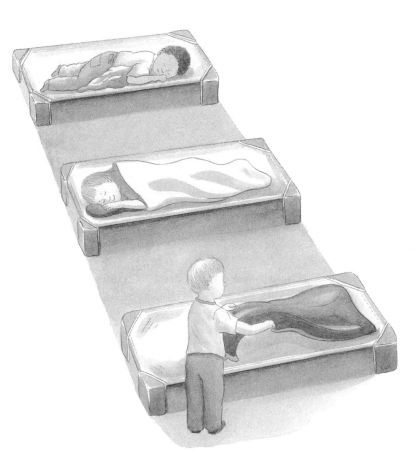

Caring and Teaching

From birth, children differ in how much sleep they need, how soundly they sleep, and the regularity of their sleeping patterns. Children also differ in the length of time they require to fall asleep and wake up. Knowing how each child falls asleep and wakes can help you manage nap time with a group of infants, toddlers, and twos. According to the National Sleep Foundation, when infants are put to bed drowsy but not asleep, they are more likely to soothe themselves, to fall asleep independently at bedtime, and to put themselves back to sleep when they wake during the night.[32] As always, talk with families about how they prefer to help their children fall asleep and follow family practices when possible.

Your Own Views

- Can you think of a bedtime ritual that you have used effectively with your own children or the children in your care? What was it? How did it make the child feel about going to sleep?

- How do you help a child feel comfortable enough to fall asleep? How do you help children transition from sleeping to reengaging in the program when they wake up?

- Why might a child cry or have difficulty falling asleep? Is there more than one reason? How does a child's crying at nap time make you feel?

- How long do you think infants, toddlers, and twos should sleep each day? Do you let children sleep until they wake up by themselves or do you wake them at a certain time? Why?

Here are some suggestions for caring and teaching during sleeping and nap times.

Learn about and follow each child's sleeping pattern. Children may not sleep at exactly the same time each day, but careful observation helps you identify and provide for their patterns. The transition to nap time for toddlers and twos should be quiet, to help them relax. Also plan for when children wake up. Provide activities for toddlers and twos who wake up while the others are still sleeping.

Know how each child in your primary care group falls asleep and wakes up. Some children fall asleep immediately, while others take longer. Some children wake up ready to go, while others prefer some quiet time before getting started. Learn each child's individual napping style so you can provide adequately for the full range of sleeping and waking styles in your room.

Develop consistent nap time routines with individual children, to help them fall asleep. Learn each child's routine for calming down, relaxing, and falling asleep. Talk with families about what they do at home so you can offer similar routines in your room. Some typical strategies are singing the same lullaby, playing a familiar CD, rocking, rubbing a child's back, or reading a story. Dimming the lights and playing soft, soothing music often help children relax.

Do not put children to sleep with a bottle. Allowing children to have a bottle in their mouths for long periods while they are sleeping may cause the severe tooth decay known as baby bottlemouth. Having bottles during nap time can also cause choking and ear infections.

Respond appropriately to children who cry at nap time. Your response to a child who cries depends in large part on your knowledge of the child. Some children cry to release tension before they fall asleep. Others cry if they are overtired or afraid. A short cry before falling asleep is normal for some children. Others need to be picked up and held in order to settle down.

Keep a sleeping log. A record of the child's active and sleeping periods will help you understand the cause of the crying and respond appropriately. You can also talk with family members, to help you understand why a child cries and to determine the best way to respond. Remember, though, that completely ignoring a crying child is never appropriate.

Take infants out of their cribs as soon as they wake up. Cribs are only for sleeping. Put babies on the floor for tummy time or provide other play experiences.

Avoid making nap time a battle. When children associate nap time with tension and stress, they are more likely to cry when you put them to sleep. Find ways to reduce your own stress and aim to enjoy the napping process with children. Keep in mind that sleeping means being still and that infants, toddlers, and twos—who are learning how to move their bodies—want to use their emerging physical skills. They may not want to be picked up, held, rocked, and placed in a crib to rest. Some children protest by standing in their cribs and crying, or by squirming in your arms as you try to rock them.

Knowing a child's temperament, wants, and needs allows you to create a nap time routine that works for him. Involve families in developing successful strategies for children who resist sleeping.

Encourage families to bring familiar comfort items from home. Giving children safe items that they use at home to comfort themselves or playing familiar music can help them relax and fall asleep.

Take children outdoors each day. Make sure that infants, toddlers, and twos have both daily exercise and sleep. Time in the fresh air and sunshine also helps to establish patterns of wakefulness and sleep.

Responding to What Children Need

Your plans and methods of managing sleeping and nap time will differ according to the ages of the children in your care and what you know about each child.

Young infants typically develop a consistent sleep-wake cycle between 3 and 6 months of age. This cycle of staying awake when it is light and going to sleep when it is dark is known as *Circadian rhythm*. Infants with an established Circadian rhythm typically sleep 9–12 hours during the night and take 30- to 120-minute naps, 1–4 times a day.[33] By the time they are age 1, they may take fewer and shorter naps during the day. Infants communicate their need for sleep by crying, rubbing their eyes, or simply falling asleep wherever they are. While sleeping, they often appear restless, twitch their arms and legs, smile, and suck.[34] As you respond to their sleep signals, you are helping them regulate their behavior.

Jasmine (8 months) has previously enjoyed being rocked to sleep for her nap. However, when Janet rocks her at nap time today, Jasmine continues to squirm and cry. Janet tries to put Jasmine down in her crib, but she cries even harder.	
Janet's Thoughts and Questions	I know that Jasmine is not hungry and that she has a clean diaper. I think she is just tired and needs a nap, but she seems to be resisting my efforts to help her fall asleep. Even though rocking is usually what she likes, it isn't working today. I wonder if her mother left a note this morning that might give me a clue.
How Janet Responds	Janet carries Jasmine to the bulletin board where family notes are posted. She finds a note and reads that Jasmine might be teething and that, although she needs more time than usual to calm down, she still reacts well to rocking. Janet decides to go back to rocking and to sing Jasmine one of her favorite lullabies. Within 5 minutes, Jasmine's body relaxes and quiets. She looks up at Janet, who is still singing.
What Jasmine Might Be Learning	To express a variety of emotions and needs by using facial expressions, body movement, and vocalizations (*Objective 1, Regulates own emotions and behaviors; Dimension c, Takes care of own needs appropriately*) To show interest in the speech of others (*Objective 8, Listens to and understands increasingly complex language; Dimension a, Comprehends language*)

Mobile infants tend to take fewer naps. They also give verbal or nonverbal signals that they need to rest. For instance, mobile infants may appear drowsy (even if they have just arrived at child care). They may cry or be irritable and difficult to comfort. Sometimes mobile infants protest strongly when you put them in their cribs, even though they are tired. When you respond consistently to their cues, you promote children's learning about nap time routines. Mobile infants begin to regulate their sleep-wake cycle to get the rest they need.

Willard (11 months) arrives at the center this morning at 7:30. He is in a good mood for a while, as he plays with playdough, trucks, and blocks. At 10:15, Grace observes that he cries every time another child comes near him. When she offers a toy or tries to involve him in another activity, he does not engage with it.	
Grace's Thoughts and Questions	Willard hasn't napped in the morning for a few weeks, but he seems tired today. I think a nap might help him. Without one, he might become overly tired and unable to eat lunch or play happily. How can I help him to relax and rest for a little while?
How Grace Responds	Grace rubs Willard's back and says, "Willard, you look tired. I think a rest might help." He does not respond. Next she offers him his favorite blanket, saying, "Here's your blankie." He looks up at Grace, raising his arms. She picks him up, takes him to the glider, sits him in her lap, rubs his back, and rocks him. He snuggles to her and closes his eyes.
What Willard Might Be Learning	To use others' facial expressions, gestures, and voices to guide his own behavior (*Objective 1, Regulates own emotions and behaviors; Dimension a, Manages feelings*) To respond to simple gestures and to the intonation, pitch, and volume of simple speech (*Objective 8, Listens to and understands increasingly complex language; Dimension a, Comprehends language*)

Toddlers and twos usually take one nap a day, lasting 1–3 hours. They communicate their need for sleep both nonverbally and verbally. Sometime during their second year, children change from sleeping in the morning and afternoon to sleeping only during the afternoon. As time passes, they may take longer to calm down and fall asleep, or they may just rest and not sleep on some days. During this time, one nap might not be enough and two might be too many. This transition can be difficult, especially in group care situations. Remain flexible and plan your day to allow for one or two nap periods per day. Plan for a quiet time to help toddlers transition from active play to sleep, and prepare experiences for children when they wake up. As you plan, remember that some children will be ready to play actively while others are still sleeping. Despite changes in their need for sleep, children still depend on you to help them regulate sleep and wakefulness.

Mercedes has put on some soft music and is sitting on the floor between two cots, gently rubbing children's backs to help them relax at nap time. In another part of the room, Matthew (22 months) is rolling around on his cot and babbling. Mercedes hears a thud and realizes that Matthew has thrown a book across the room.	
Mercedes' Thoughts and Questions	Every day this week, Matthew has had difficulty relaxing and falling asleep. Even when I put him in a quiet corner alone, he manages to disrupt the other children. How can I help Matthew and the other children in my room at the same time?
How Mercedes Responds	Matthew continues to roll on his cot, so Mercedes walks quietly across the room and softly says to him, "I can see that you are tired of this book, but when you throw books someone might get hurt." She offers Matthew a soft book and a cloth bunny. She tells him that he may play with them until she returns. "When I come back, I will read a story to you," she says. He says, "Yeah, book" and begins looking at the book while he talks to the bunny.
What Matthew Might Be Learning	To respond to simple directions and sometimes test limits (*Objective 1, Regulates own emotions and behaviors; Dimension b, Follow limits and expectations*) To speak in two-word phrases (*Objective 9, Uses language to express thoughts and needs; Dimension c, Uses conventional grammar*)

Working in Partnership With Families

Working with families to provide consistency between home and your center is essential for helping children establish good sleeping and nap time habits. Here are some suggestions for working with families to make sleeping a positive experience for children in your room and at home.

Gather information about children's sleeping habits and patterns. Develop an Individual Care Plan with families at the time of enrollment. Update it on a regular basis by asking families how many hours a night their children sleep. Find out about children's sleeping schedules. Learn about the families' bedtime rituals and routines.

Share information about sleeping on a daily basis as well. When children do not follow their typical napping schedule and sleep less than usual, be sure to let parents know. The information will enable them to recognize crankiness or other troublesome behavior as a sign of tiredness and adjust bedtime accordingly. When a child has extended her nap time, inform her family that she has had a long nap and is rested. Knowing this, her family member may decide to vary their routine on the way home.

Be aware of families' cultural preferences for putting infants, toddlers, and twos to sleep. Some families may not put children to sleep in a separate room. They may not let children sleep alone and may keep them awake until older children in the household go to sleep. Infants in some cultures may be swaddled or put to sleep on bedboards. Become knowledgeable about the sleeping practices your families follow with their children, and, whenever possible and appropriate, incorporate them into your program.

Work together to resolve differences. Some families may ask you to limit the time their child sleeps at your program. Listen and gather information from family members. Share information about your views and teaching experience, and then work out a plan that is acceptable for both your room and their home. As you strive to reach agreement, keep an open mind about new possibilities that evolve as you talk with each other.

Offer support to families. Be available to support families whose children have sleeping problems. Reassure them that sleeping problems are common, especially during the first years of life. Take time to read and stay current with new information about sleeping issues and practices for young children. Ideas about best practices change over time, and you want to be sure that the information you give to parents is up-to-date. Encourage families to talk with other families whose children are having similar sleeping problems. They might be able to share helpful suggestions. Remind family members that each child has his own style of sleeping and waking, and that differences are natural and expected and are not necessarily signs of a problem.

The letter to families that follows is another way to share information.

Dear Families:

Every young child needs enough sleep during the day and at night for healthy growth and development. When children are rested, they enjoy and benefit from learning opportunities throughout the day. When your baby was born, you may have expected him to sleep easily. Many babies do, but sleeping is sometimes difficult for others. Your infant needs you to figure out how to comfort him and help him relax into sleep. As his needs and preferences change when he gets older, it will still be very important for you to respond to his changing patterns. Sharing information will help us make sure that the sleeping routine we offer at the program is consistent with the care you provide at home.

How We Can Work Together

- **Let us know your child's preferences.** We are helped by knowing what works or does not work at home. Does your baby fall asleep quickly, or does she take some time? Is there a special lullaby you sing or words your child is used to hearing at bedtime?

- **Keep us informed about any changes in your child's sleeping patterns.** When we know that your child's pattern has changed at home, we can adapt his schedule at the program. We will share the same information with you so we can both plan better. For example, if we know that your child did not sleep well the night before, we can offer an early nap if necessary. If you know your child took a long nap and is well rested, you may decide to vary your routine instead of going straight home. Please let us know if you have concerns about your child's sleeping schedule at our program. For instance, please tell us if you think he is sleeping too little or too much.

- **Bring special items that comfort your child.** If your child has a special blanket or other object that makes falling asleep easier, please bring it to the center. Please label it with your child's name and make sure we have it every day. We will take care that it does not get lost and help you remember to take it home at night.

- **Always put your baby to sleep on his or her back.** This is a recommendation of the American Academy of Pediatrics to help prevent Sudden Infant Death Syndrome, or SIDS. You can check on the latest recommendations of the American Academy of Pediatrics by reading their Web site or asking us for this information. We will be happy to share what we have learned with you.

We appreciate your help. Together, we can help make sleeping and nap time a pleasant and restful experience for your child.

Sincerely,

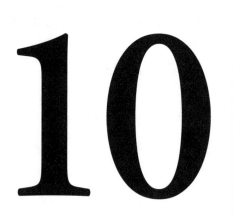

10 Getting Dressed

Supporting Development and Learning 244

Creating an Environment for Getting Dressed 245

Caring and Teaching 246
Responding to What Children Need 249
Working in Partnership With Families 252

Sharing Thoughts About Getting Dressed 253

Getting Dressed

Brooks is about to dress Abby (14 months). She starts by playing peek-a-boo with Abby's shirt. Hiding her face behind the shirt, Brooks playfully pretends to worry, "I can't see Abby! Where is Abby?" While Abby giggles in response, Brooks gently slides the shirt over her head and says, "There she is! First we put your head through and then your arms." Abby cooperates by extending her arms, as Brooks offers one armhole and then the other. "Thank you for helping me put your shirt on," Brooks says. Abby then holds up a sock, and Brooks asks, "Where does the sock go?" Abby smiles broadly and touches her foot. "Right, it goes on your foot."

Infants, toddlers, and twos are totally dependent on adults to provide for their basic needs. One basic need is clothing. Meeting this need includes dressing children in clothes that are clean and dry and that are appropriate for the weather and for both indoor and outdoor play.

Dressing and undressing children are simple yet repetitive activities that can become tiresome when approached as tasks to be completed quickly. Changing clothing may even become a struggle when a child resists you or insists on doing it herself. By approaching dressing and undressing as troublesome chores rather than as learning opportunities, you miss chances to enjoy being with a child and encourage new skills.

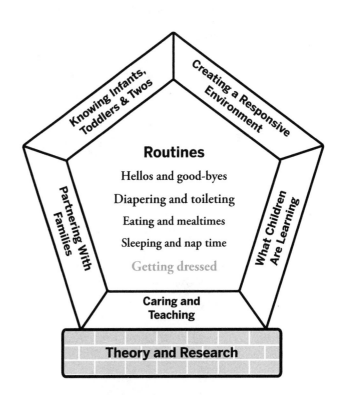

Supporting Development and Learning

Dressing and undressing can be rich experiences for children when they are viewed as opportunities to develop social–emotional, physical, cognitive, and communication skills.

Learning about themselves and others: Off go the shoes. Over the head goes the shirt. Down go the pants. Snap goes the jacket. Dressing and undressing routines are chances for infants, toddlers, and twos to begin to learn personal care skills. Competence and pride in accomplishment grow as each new skill emerges. The "do-every-thing-for-me-baby" quickly becomes the "I-can-do-it-myself" 2-year-old who can take over parts of his own care.

Learning about moving: During dressing and undressing, children use small and large muscles. A mobile infant who holds her foot in the air so you can put on her sock, or who pushes her arm through an armhole, is coordinating her body and increasing her physical strength. When a 2-year-old repeatedly puts on and takes off his jacket, he is using a sequence of physical skills. Getting the jacket on with the over-the-head method requires full body movement, while attempts at zipping, snapping, and eventually buttoning involve small muscles.

Learning about the world: For a toddler or two to find his two matching shoes among all of the shoes under the coat hooks, he must see similarities and differences as well as remember, recognize, and classify objects by the characteristics of color, shape, and size. Giving toddlers and twos time to find their shoes by themselves is an early exercise in memory, sorting, and matching. A child who points to his jacket on the coat hook when you say, "It's time to go outdoors," is thinking ahead and planning. When you say, "It's cold outside today," and he takes his mittens out of his pocket and tries to put them on, he is beginning to use problem solving strategies. When you allow enough time for getting dressed, you are inviting children to learn about the world and to increase their ability to function in it.

Learning about communicating: By naming body parts and items of clothing while you are dressing a child, you teach new words. Your conversations with infants while you are putting on their pants, with toddlers while you are helping zip their jackets, or with twos when you are tying their shoes supports their understanding and use of language. Reading books about dressing also helps extend their most basic language skills by introducing details related to dressing and items of clothing. For instance, in *Corduroy*, by Don Freeman, Lisa's stuffed bear loses the button from his overalls, and she sews it back on his shoulder strap.

Creating an Environment for Getting Dressed

The arrangement of your room and the materials you provide can help infants, toddlers, and twos participate in dressing and undressing. A few simple additions can engage children in a variety of motor experiences that support their eye-hand coordination, an awareness of their own bodies in space, and their ability to sequence tasks.

Store children's personal clothing items within their reach. Provide coat hooks, cubbies, and storage containers for items that children can safely get on their own. Storage that is out of their reach may be used for items that children do not need to retrieve regularly. When personal items such as coats, jackets, and spare clothing are accessible to toddlers and twos, they are encouraged throughout the day to dress independently. The American Academy of Pediatrics and the American Public Health Association recommend that coat hooks be placed either slightly above or below children's eye level to minimize risk of injury to eyes, and that the hooks be spaced or put in individual cubbies so that coats will not touch each other.[35]

Bag soiled clothing; do not wash or rinse it. Washing or rinsing clothing increases the risk of contamination for teachers and other children. Put each child's soiled clothing in a separate plastic bag, close the bag securely, and send the clothing home at pick-up time.

Label storage places for personal clothing so that children can begin to find their own things. Putting picture or photo labels of children on cubbies or next to hooks makes it easy for teachers, children, and families to recognize where each child's personal items belong and to put them in the same place each day.

Supply dress-up clothing and other materials for practicing dressing skills. Select dress-up clothing that is easy to put on and take off so children can have fun practicing. To minimize frustration, be prepared to assist when necessary. Items such as vests with snaps, shoes with laces or Velcro®, and jackets and shirts with buttons or zippers encourage children to learn snapping, buttoning, lacing, and zipping. Add an unbreakable mirror so children can see themselves in their fancy vests and oversized shoes and enjoy the results of dressing themselves. The National Association for the Education of Young Children recommends that, unless disposable hats are used, hats be cleaned after each use. They also advise washing dress-up clothing weekly.[36] In addition to dress-up clothing, boards with fasteners and old shoes with buckles or laces give children chances to practice dressing skills. In fact, virtually all items that engage children in small muscle activity are helpful.

Caring and Teaching

Dressing times may seem like the most ordinary of all the daily routines in caring for young children. It is tempting to want to get through the process as quickly as possible, especially when trying to change a squirming, crying baby or a toddler or 2-year-old who wants to do everything by himself. If you take the time to pay attention to each child during dressing times, this routine offers many opportunities to interact with the child and to build a child's sense of competence.

Your Own Views

- How do you feel when a child protests about getting dressed? How do you help minimize protests and make getting dressed as easy and as comfortable as possible for both you and the child?

- Do you make suggestions to families about what their children should wear to your program? How do you feel when families do not follow your suggestions? Can you think of some reasons why they do not follow your advice?

- Do you believe a child should dress himself? If so, at what age do you think children should have the skills for dressing?

Here are some practical suggestions for making dressing routines work well for you and the children.

Handle children's bodies with respect. When you touch or pick up an infant, consider how you handle her body. Do you lift her swiftly into the air and then quickly lay her down on the diaper-changing table? Do you stop, bend beside her, smile, tell her that you are going to pick her up, let her know you need her help, and then pause and wait for her reaction before gently lifting her up? By interacting gently throughout the dressing process, you let infants, toddlers, and twos know that you respect their bodies. When lifting young infants, remember to support their heads and necks.

Talk with children about what you are doing. Use caring words and a calm voice while changing children's clothes. Describe what you are doing as you do it. "I will put your head through this part…Your arm goes in here…There it is! Your clean shirt is right on your tummy!" Be playful. Ask a toddler or 2-year-old, "Where should we put your sock? Does it go on your head? No-o-o. That's silly. It goes on your foot." Learn the words in children's home languages for common articles of clothing so you can use them as you dress or undress the child.

Be aware that children's temperaments influence the way they experience dressing. Some children have intense reactions to wet clothing or any change in the condition of their clothing. Others are more flexible and easygoing and do not seem to be bothered if their shirts are wet or sticky. Some children need you to help them move quickly through the dressing process. Others do better when you slow down and take your time. For children who are sensitive to touch and find certain textures uncomfortable, you will want to have soft, tagless, well-worn cotton clothing on hand.

Let children participate in whatever way they can. An infant may simply lift his arm when you put a shirt on him, while a 2-year-old might put a sweater on with only a little assistance. Observe how each child in your group prefers to participate, and adjust your approach to involve each child as much as possible.

Keep familiar extra clothing on hand for each child. Ask families to bring clothing from home so their children can be changed when necessary during the day. Also keep an ample supply of extra clothing in your room to be shared as needed. You can ask for donations from all parents, shop at garage sales or similar places, or save leftover and forgotten clothing from year to year.

Give children choices whenever possible. Simple choices provide them with a much-needed sense of control and with practice in making decisions. You may ask mobile infants, toddlers, and twos a simple question such as, "Are you ready to go with me?" Then pause to watch for their reaction. Ask 2-year-olds more complex questions and wait for their responses: "Do you want to get dressed here by your cot or over there by your cubby?" "Do you want to wear your green socks with butterflies or the purple ones?"

Engage children with songs, fingerplays, and playful games that encourage learning and cooperation. When you dress a young infant who is lying on his back, lean slightly forward so that he can focus on your face as you sing and talk. One day you can sing a line such as, "This is the way we put on your shirt." Substitute *pants, shoes, socks,* and *jacket* on other days. Involve toddlers and twos by asking them to help choose the game they would like to play, song to sing, or fingerplay to say as they dress. Do not hesitate to repeat favorite games, songs, and fingerplays that children enjoy. Use them as long as they help children participate or remain calm. When you find that they are not helpful, choose another strategy.

Step in to minimize frustration when a child attempts a task that might be too difficult to accomplish alone. Recognize that children are eager to help with dressing and may want to help even when a task is too difficult for them. Stay nearby and offer help as needed. When a child is becoming frustrated, be ready to offer comfort and reassurance. "Buttoning that button is tricky. May I help?" "That zipper seems to be stuck. Maybe we can get it up if both of us try." When a child makes a mistake, offer a new way to look at the situation. For example, when a toddler or 2-year-old has put his shoes on the wrong feet, you might say, "You did it all by yourself! How do those shoes feel? If we switched them, would they feel different? Let's try that and see."

Responding to What Children Need

Depending upon their temperaments and developmental levels, children react to dressing very differently. Vary your approaches according to what you know about each child.

Young infants interact with you one-on-one during dressing. When Linda changes Julio's clothing, he explores his environment by looking around and listening. As she sings and talks to him in gentle tones, he explores his world. He focuses on Linda's face; visually searches the room to identify the sources of sounds; and moves his hands and feet, learning where his body ends and the rest of the world begins. He experiments with his voice, cooing softly, gurgling, and squealing. Before long, he begins to participate in dressing by extending a leg for a sock and by pushing his arms through armholes.

Linda is feeding Julio (4 months) a bottle. When he finishes, she rocks him, and he becomes drowsy. As she lays him in his crib, she notices that the neck of his sleeper is wet under his chin. However, he does not seem to mind and falls asleep immediately.	
Linda's Thoughts and Questions	Julio's sleeper is wet. I know that keeping him clean and dry is important. Should I wake him to change his sleeper now, or let him sleep and change it when he wakes?
How Linda Responds	Linda checks to see how much of Julio's sleeper is wet and whether he is chilled. She decides to wait until he wakes up and to change his sleeper when she changes his diaper.
What Julio Might Be Learning	To develop routine patterns for sleeping and other basic needs, with adult's help (*Objective 1, Regulates own emotions and behaviors; Dimension c, Takes care of own needs appropriately*)

Mobile infants may cooperate as you dress them. You may also witness their emerging sense of independence as they take off clothing frequently during the day, especially their socks and shoes. Celebrate their accomplishments before you put their clothes back on. A simple acknowledgment of their success is helpful in supporting their development, as when you say, "You took your socks off all by yourself!"

Brooks hears Abby (14 months) squeal with delight. Brooks looks across the room and sees Abby toddling across the carpet. She has a shoe on one foot. The other is bare. When Brooks notices Abby's sock and shoe nearby, she realizes that Abby removed them.	
Brooks' Thoughts and Questions	Abby seems to be enjoying herself and her accomplishments. I realize that learning to dress and undress is important, but one of her feet is bare and the floor is a little cold.
	I know Abby will probably protest and resist my attempts to put her sock and shoe back on.
	How can I help her put them back on without a power struggle?
How Brooks Responds	Brooks picks up Abby's shoe and sock. She approaches Abby with both in hand and playfully crawls beside her on the floor.
	As Brooks crawls, she sings, "Where is Abby? Where is Abby? She's missing her sock and her shoe. Where is Abby? Where is Abby? She's missing her sock and her shoe." Abby laughs. Brooks laughs and cuddles her while slipping on her sock and shoe.
What Abby Might Be Learning	To use others' facial expressions, gestures, or voices to guide own behavior (*Objective 2, Establishes and sustains positive relationships; Dimension b, Responds to emotional cues*)
	To attempt simple personal care tasks (*Objective 1, Regulates own emotions and behaviors; Dimension c, Takes care of own needs appropriately*)

Toddlers and twos are developing the skills they need to put on and take off simple clothing by themselves. They gain confidence in their abilities when you take note of their accomplishments. Toddlers and twos may insist, "Me do it!" when you attempt to help them. They may also try to assert control or independence by playing a game of chase when you want to dress them. Remember that they are not trying to make your life difficult. They are trying to take charge of themselves.

Mercedes helps the children in her room get ready to go outside. They put on their coats, hats, and gloves. Everyone is ready to go except Matthew (22 months), who has his hat and coat on but is struggling with his zipper. Mercedes approaches Matthew, kneels down, and asks, "Matthew, may I help you with your zipper?" Matthew says, "No," and turns away.

Mercedes' Thoughts and Questions	I know that Matthew likes to do things by himself, but the rest of the group is ready to go outside. I want to support Matthew's desire to do things on his own, but I don't want the other children to have to wait too long. I know that, if I don't do something to gain his cooperation, this situation could turn into a power struggle. How can I support Matthew's independence and avoid a power struggle while helping him get his coat zipped?
How Mercedes Responds	Mercedes gently touches Matthew's arm and says, "Matthew, will you please help me zip my coat?" Matthew turns around and looks at her coat. As she begins zipping, Mercedes says, "I'll start at the bottom. Will you finish zipping it all the way up for me?" Matthew smiles and zips her coat. "Zzzzip!" responds Mercedes, exaggerating the word. Matthew laughs. "Now, how about your coat? I'll start the zipper, and then you can zip it all the way up." Matthew agrees. As he zips his coat, he repeats Mercedes' exaggerated, "Zzzzip!"
What Matthew Might Be Learning	To try more complex personal care tasks, with increasing success (*Objective 1, Regulates own emotions and behaviors; Dimension c, Takes care of own needs appropriately*) To use eye-hand coordination while doing simple tasks (*Objective 7, Demonstrates fine-motor strength and coordination; Dimension a, Uses fingers and hands*) To demonstrate understanding of simple directions, questions, and explanations (*Objective 8, Listens to and understands increasingly complex language; Dimension b, Follows directions*)

Working in Partnership With Families

At home, families probably experience many of the same joys and struggles you have while dressing their child. Share your ideas for successful dressing experiences and ask for their help. Talk with families about how they manage dressing at home. The "Individual Care Plan— Family Information Form" includes a place to record information that families share about dressing. You can incorporate some of their regular practices into your dressing routine. For example, you might want to follow a mother's practice of dressing her baby while sitting on the floor rather than while at the changing table.

Let families know what they need to provide for their child, such as ample extra clothing that is labeled with their child's name. Request that they dress their children in clothing that allows them to be active and sometimes get messy. Assure families that you will help their children take care of their clothing by providing smocks for art and for water play.

As the weather changes, be sure to remind families which articles of clothing the children will need for safe and active outdoor play. Depending upon the climate where you live, this might mean warm jackets, mittens, hats, and boots in winter, and loose clothing and sun hats in summer. Sending a letter like the sample that follows is one way of engaging families as partners in dressing their children.

Dear Families:

Infants, toddlers, and twos are dressed and undressed throughout the day—every day—at home and in our program. Dressing is one routine that adults and children often want to finish as quickly as possible. After all, dressing a squirming infant, a protesting toddler, or a 2-year-old who insists on putting on her own clothes is not a simple task. From the child's point of view, stopping what she is doing and being still while an adult dresses her is not fun, either.

We view the dressing routine as rich in learning possibilities and as an opportunity to focus on one child at a time. As we pull on a shirt or pants, we talk, listen, sing, and play a simple game. We offer children choices, letting them select which shirt to wear or which item of clothing to put on first. By asking rather than telling, we reduce the struggles we might otherwise have and engage the children in helping us instead.

How We Can Work Together

- **Please provide extra articles of clothing.** We want your child to be warm enough or cool enough, dry, and as clean as possible. Spare clothes that your child is used to wearing help us keep your child comfortable. When extra clothing is labeled with your child's name, we have time to interact with your child because we do not need to spend it to figure out which clothes belong to whom. Remember that, as your child grows and as seasons change, you will need to replace the extra clothes you have left with us.

- **Select clothing that is easy to manage.** Pants with elastic waists, shoes with Velcro® fasteners, and overalls with straps that stretch make getting dressed easier for your child and for us.

- **Share ideas with us about dressing your child.** Let us know what works well when you dress your child at home. We will let you know what works for us, too. By sharing ideas, we can learn from one another and strengthen our partnership to benefit your child.

- **Dress your child for active, sometimes messy play.** Also be sure that your child's clothes are appropriate for the weather. That way, playing outside will be healthy and pleasurable. Remember that clothes with a snug fit or that need to be kept clean prevent children from fully enjoying such activities as climbing, food preparation, and painting. If you want to bring your child to our program in clothes that you do not want to become soiled, we'll be happy to help him or her change into play clothes that do not restrict movement or handling messy materials. We will do our best to take care of your child's clothes.

Together, we can make getting dressed a positive learning experience for your child.

Sincerely,

Part B
Experiences

Children whose basic needs have been met consistently and who have secure attachments are eager to experience the world. According to Jean Piaget, infants and toddlers learn through **sensorimotor activity**. They react to what they experience through their senses and through physical activity. For example, they discover that they can make a noise by banging a toy, that objects fall when they are dropped, and that a ball rolls when pushed. During the **preoperational stage**, which starts around age 2, children continue to explore objects and begin to use them purposefully. They stack blocks until they fall, fit shapes in a sorting box, use a crayon to make marks, and use objects in pretend play.

Caring for infants, toddlers, and twos is deeply satisfying when you appreciate and find joy in the everyday discoveries that delight a child: the sound a rattle makes, a clown that pops up when a button is pressed, the ants marching across the pavement. You plan meaningful experiences for infants, toddlers, and twos by selecting materials that match children's growing abilities and interests, by observing what children do, and by thinking about what you learn. Because you can never predict exactly how children will react and what will capture their attention, you *plan for possibilities*. Your positive interactions make children's experiences opportunities for building relationships and promoting learning. Lev Vygotsky emphasized this social dimension of learning.

The chapters in Part B describe how each type of experience supports children's development and learning. Each chapter also suggests appropriate materials for each age-group and explains how you can support children's learning by thoughtfully observing and responding to each child. The letter that concludes each chapter will help you explain the value of the experience to children's families. The letters are also available from www.TeachingStrategies.com/it2-forms. You may use them as they were written or adapt them as necessary for your program.

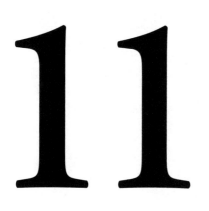

Playing With Toys

Supporting Development and Learning 258

Creating an Environment for Playing With Toys 259
Selecting Materials for Different Ages 260
Including All Children 264
Setting Up and Displaying Materials 265

Caring and Teaching 266
Responding to and Planning for Each Child 269

Sharing Thoughts About the Value of Toys 273

Playing With Toys

Brooks shakes a covered shoe box to show Abby (14 months) that something is inside. Opening her mouth in surprise, Brooks prompts, "I wonder what's making that noise." Abby reaches for the box and pulls off the lid. Inside is a collection of large, colorful, plastic laundry detergent bottle tops that Brooks has saved. Abby reaches in with both hands and picks up two bottle tops. She looks them over, bangs them together a few times, and then tosses them onto the rug. Several more times, she reaches into the box with one hand, grasps another top, and throws it. "You really like to throw those bottle tops," Brooks comments. With a big smile, Abby dumps the rest of the tops out of the box and claps her hands.

Some of the very best playthings for infants, toddlers, and twos are not commercial toys. They are simply common objects and natural materials that appeal to children and that can be explored safely. Large plastic bottle tops, cardboard boxes, crinkly tissue paper, wooden and plastic kitchen utensils, pinecones, leaves, and shells appeal to young children as much as many toys you can purchase (and sometimes even more). Any object that young children can explore, put together, take apart, push or pull, stack, or bang becomes a toy in a child's hands.

Many toys are designed to entertain children and capture their attention, for example, mobiles that swing and play music and wind-up toys that move across the floor. Other toys are structured to fit together in a particular way: puzzles, nesting cups, and pegboards. Still others are open-ended and can be used in a variety of ways: to build and stack, or to create a pattern or design.

All toys must meet safety standards so that children under age 3 can explore them safely with all of their senses. Effective toys capture children's attention, keep them engaged, and help them acquire and strengthen new skills.

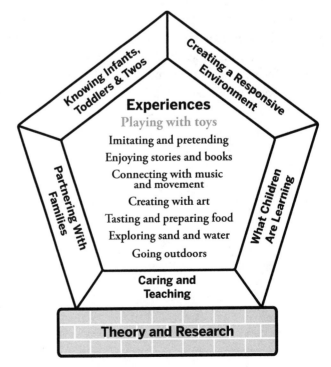

Supporting Development and Learning

Infants, toddlers, and twos develop social–emotional, physical, cognitive, and language skills when they play with toys.

Learning about themselves and others: As young children develop a trusting relationship with you, they become more confident about exploring toys. They experiment and are eager to see your reactions. Toys that can be used successfully by more than one person—such as balls, blocks, and simple matching games—teach children about the give-and-take of relationships and how to recognize the needs of others.

Learning about moving: Toys inspire young children to explore actively. As they grasp, pull apart, fit together, fill and dump, stack, roll, and toss toys, children are strengthening and refining the small muscles in their hands and fingers and developing eye-hand coordination. They develop large-muscle skills as they carry toys, build with blocks, and push and pull toys such as wagons and small brooms.

Learning about the world: Children learn how objects can be used by exploring the toys you provide. They learn that a rattle will make a noise only if they move it and that a round block will only fit through a round hole, not a square one, if the hole is the same size as the block. When an infant pushes a button on a toy and it makes music, and if the child repeats the action again and again with the same result, she learns about cause and effect. Trying several ways to fit the pieces of a puzzle together helps children develop problem-solving strategies. Children's ability to sustain attention grows as they explore what they can do with toys. Beads, blocks, large pegs, Duplos® and other manipulatives provide opportunities for children to explore the many ways that objects can be grouped.

Learning about communicating: Your room is filled with interesting objects, such as a big red block, a soft squishy bear, and a round bouncing ball. As you direct children's attention to toys, name them, and describe their characteristics, you teach children interesting language. Toys that are appealing and fun for children inspire conversations, especially if you show an interest in what children are doing, describe what your senses tell you, and ask questions. When you hear an infant say, "Ba, ba," as he plays with a ball, you know he is connecting the word with the appropriate object and learning to express his ideas.

Creating an Environment for Playing With Toys

Offer children an assortment of simple toys that vary in color. Include some that are open-ended so children can use them in different ways. As always, children's safety and health should be the primary consideration in selecting toys for children of all ages.

Keeping Children Safe and Healthy

In selecting toys for infants, toddlers, and twos, ask yourself the following questions:

- Is it solid and without breakable parts; sharp or jagged edges; or exposed nails, wires, pins, or splinters?

- Is it made of washable, nontoxic materials?

- Is it too large to be swallowed (at least 1 1/2 inches in diameter) and free of parts that might break off and become lodged in noses, ears, or windpipes?

- Are dolls' heads and limbs secure? Are facial features molded, rather than sewn on?

- Is it free of cords and strings that could become wound around a child's neck? All cords and strings must be less than 8 inches long.

- Is it stable and free of parts that could pinch or pierce children or trap their hair or clothing?

- Are hinges and joints covered?

- If made of cloth, is it nonflammable or flame-retardant (not merely flame-resistant)?

Selecting Materials for Different Ages

The ages, developmental abilities, and individual interests of children are important considerations in selecting the best toys.[37]

Young Infants

Young infants respond to toys they can see, hear, taste, touch, and smell. They focus their attention on toys and other objects that resemble a face, have clear lines, or are brightly colored. Almost every object they grasp goes directly into their mouths. When they can sit up, young infants enjoy toys that they can bat. Here are some good toys for young infants.

Mobiles—Mobiles promote the development of vision and hearing when infants are interested in the sight and sound of them. Infants especially like mobiles with patterns, circles, and high contrast, and those that make music. Hang a mobile over a play area, about 14 inches from their eyes, where they can focus best. At about 4 months, infants will begin to reach for the mobile, so you will need to move it higher to keep them from pulling it down.

Mirrors—From the age of about 4–6 months, children are captivated by mirrors. Watching their image appear and disappear in a mirror helps them learn to focus. You can position stable, unbreakable mirrors on the bottom of walls in play spaces where infants can enjoy looking at their images.

Cuddly toys—Stuffed animals; hand puppets; and soft, washable, one-piece rag dolls delight young infants and help them begin to learn concepts like *hard–soft*, *light–dark*, and *big–little*. Bright colors, boldly contrasting patterns, painted faces, and sounds are more important at this early age than realistic features.

Grasping and mouthing toys—From about 3 months on, young infants love to grasp, shake, mouth, drop, and explore objects that they can hold in their fists. These include small rattles, teethers, plastic key rings with keys, grasping balls, and cloth toys.

Mobile Infants

Mobile infants continue to enjoy toys that they can explore with all of their senses.

> **Willard** (11 months) finds that a large stuffed dinosaur is easier to hug than a small rubber one. As **Abby** (14 months) yanks on large snap beads or inserts a circle into a foam board, she learns how to squeeze, twist, push, and pull.

Puzzles, block towers, and large pegs in a pegboard are great fun to take apart, although a mobile infant may not yet be able to put them together. Here is a list of toys for mobile infants.

Balls—A ball is one of the toys that children love most. They delight in rolling, holding, getting, and throwing balls of all types. Provide a variety of sizes and textures, such as clutch balls with easily grasped, indented surfaces; balls with chimes or visible objects rolling inside; and balls that roll in unpredictable ways, such as weighted balls and oddly shaped ones. When they can stand, mobile infants enjoy the challenge of batting a large beach ball.

Manipulative toys—These are toys that mobile infants can pull apart and fit together, dump and fill, stack and knock down, and shake. Good selections are stacking rings, nesting cups, foam boards, shape sorters, and measuring spoons.

Puzzles—For mobile infants, select puzzles with only two or three pieces and with pieces that can be held by knobs. (You can glue empty spools on the pieces to serve as knobs if they do not come that way.) The puzzles should be colorful and depict objects, people, or animals familiar to the child. By exploring the puzzle pieces and discovering how the shapes fit together, mobile infants develop eye-hand coordination and problem-solving strategies.

Activity boxes—These toys have doors that open, dials to turn, knobs to pull, and buttons to push. They can be attached to furniture and provide practice in wrist control and the use of finger muscles. Examples are busy boxes and surprise boxes that pop up.

Push-and-pull toys—Sturdy carriages and child-size shopping carts are especially appropriate for children who are beginning to walk, because they offer much-needed support. More experienced walkers enjoy such toys as plastic lawn mowers and carpet sweepers. Toys that play music or make other sounds as they move enhance the play experience by encouraging the child to move in order to make the sound. Such toys also help children build understandings about cause and effect.

Transportation toys—Small plastic or wooden cars, buses, trains, trucks, and airplanes delight mobile infants as they turn the wheels and push them across the floor. Ride-on toys that they scoot with their feet are exciting for this age-group when they are more balanced and coordinated.

Blocks—At first, mobile infants prefer to pick up, pile, knock down, and even throw blocks. For these reasons, foam, cloth-covered, and small plastic blocks are the best choices. Later, introduce firmer blocks, made of lightweight wood, for stacking. Stacking blocks should be cube-shaped, brightly colored or patterned, and easily grasped (2–4 inches). A selection of 20–25 blocks is sufficient.

Toddlers

Toddlers continue to use all of the toys mobile infants use, but they are likely to use them in different ways.

> **Matthew** (22 months) enjoys stacking blocks to make a tower, knocking it down, and repeating this process again and again. Sometimes he also pretends that a block is something else, like a car zooming along the road.

In order to continue supporting children's development, select toys that stimulate toddlers' understanding of themselves in relationship to the world around them. Here are some suggestions.

Push-and-pull toys—These are ideal for toddlers, who are now steady on their feet. They enjoy pushing a carriage full of dolls, mopping and sweeping with child-size tools, and pulling a wagon. These activities often lead to pretend play.

Animal figures—Soft, fuzzy stuffed animals are popular with toddlers, as are rubber, wood, vinyl, and plastic figures. They like to carry stuffed toys around and to make up scenes using farm and zoo animals and monsters.

Puzzles and matching games—These toys provide opportunities for toddlers to develop and apply thinking skills. Select simple 4- to 5-piece puzzles in which each piece is a complete picture and has a knob for children to grasp. They can be made of any thick, durable, nontoxic material.

Manipulative toys—These include more complex and challenging shape-sorting and activity boxes, nesting cups, pegboards with large pegs, stacking rings (with 5–10 pieces), and large plastic snap beads.

Transportation toys—Plastic, wooden, and metal cars, trucks, buses, trains, and airplanes continue to delight toddlers, who line them up or race them across the floor. Include some vehicles with simple movable parts, such as doors that open and close, and trains that couple easily.

Blocks—Toddlers enjoy building with a variety of lightweight but sturdy blocks. Choose blocks of uniform sizes and of shapes that are easy for children to build with and stack. Here are good choices for this age-group:

- rectangular plastic blocks of a variety of colors
- cardboard blocks designed to look like bricks and with a coating that makes them easy to clean
- large foam blocks
- large interlocking plastic blocks (such as Duplos®)
- colored wooden table-blocks of uniform sizes
- alphabet blocks

Gross-motor toys and equipment—Toys and space for gross-motor play are important, especially on days when children may not go outside. Include tunnels for toddlers to crawl through, doll carriages and child-sized shopping carts to push, and ride-on equipment that they can propel with their feet.

Twos

Twos are acquiring many new fine-motor skills, so they can manipulate objects with more purpose. They build and create with objects, sort and match materials, fit things together, arrange them in patterns and designs, and use toys for pretending. Most of the toys listed for toddlers are also of interest to twos, although they use them in more advanced ways. In addition, they are ready for more complex materials and equipment. Here are some suggestions.

Puzzles and matching games—Twos who enjoy puzzles may want the challenge of puzzles with 6–12 pieces. As they become more skilled in sorting and matching, they can play games in which they match giant dominoes (2–4 inches in size) or match simple and familiar picture pieces to lotto boards.

Manipulative toys—Twos may enjoy stringing large wooden beads on laces; lacing cards or a wooden shoe; and practicing with personal care boards that have snaps, buttons, laces, zippers, and Velcro® strips. Include more challenging shape sorters, shapes that fit together, and large plastic or wooden nuts and bolts.

Transportation toys—With their increased fine-motor skills, twos enjoy handling movable parts: steering wheels that turn; bulldozer shovels that pick up and dump; cherry pickers that they can raise and lower; and knobs, levers, buttons, and wheels of all sorts.

Unit blocks—To build stable constructions, twos need heavier, sturdier blocks. Hardwood unit blocks are the universal favorites because of their weight, durability, and many uses. While twos do not need the specialized shapes that preschoolers enjoy (such as triangles and arches), you should provide at least 40–60 blocks per builder in a group.

Simple props—Enhance the block play of 2-year-olds by including small wooden and plastic animals and people, miniature traffic signs, doll house furniture, and small vehicles. They can use them to decorate their block structures and for dramatic play.

Large blocks—Twos like to build with hollow blocks and those made of heavy cardboard or sturdy foam. They are likely to use their constructions as play settings, climbing on them, sitting inside, and pretending.

Gross-motor toys—To provide physical challenges, include climbers and riding toys that children can push with their feet. As they near age 3, some children are even able to manage tricycle pedals. Large cardboard boxes make wonderful spaces for crawling. Balls of varying shapes, colors, textures, and sizes are great for kicking, batting, throwing, and catching.

Including All Children

All children benefit from playing with toys when they are able to use them well. Depending on the disability, some toys present special challenges. You can choose toys and adapt others so that no child spends large parts of the day observing the play of others instead of actively joining in. Simple adaptations can open a world of play and exploration for children with varying types and degrees of disability. You may also find that toys chosen for a child with a disability become favorites of other children in your program.

Some easily implemented, low-technology modifications to materials and your environment can make all the difference. Here are some suggestions.[38]

Handles or built-up knobs—Glue knobs or corks to puzzles and other toys to assist children with limited fine-motor skills. Add foam curlers to build up the handles of spoons, brushes, crayons, and markers.

Activity frames—Activity frames are similar to the play "gyms" designed for infants. Hang toys securely from the frame so that the children have easy access to them. These devices allow children with motor impairments to use toys that would otherwise be out of reach or that the children would not be able to retrieve if dropped. The frames can be placed on the floor, attached to a table, or attached to a wheelchair or stander.

Playboards—You can attach toys to a firm surface (such as foam core, pegboard, or carpet) with Velcro®, string, or elastic. Create a variety of playboards that enable children to participate in imaginative play. Examples of simple playboards include a purse (with keys, brush, wallet, etc.); a tea party (with cups and spoons); or a playhouse (with people and furniture). The child can then use his hands or a grasping aid to move the pieces without worrying about dropping them. Other children can also participate in this play.

Other strategies to help children with special needs are to attach play materials to steady surfaces, to select toys with large pieces (such as puzzles), and to simplify the game or toy. Ivan has found that he just needs to provide a wedge for Gena (30 months) so she can reach and play with the toys she enjoys.

Remember that the child's family and therapists are great resources. Invite the child's physical or occupational therapist to visit your program and suggest ways to adapt your space and toys to meet the child's abilities and interests.

Setting Up and Displaying Materials

Toys should be placed near, comfortable surfaces with enough space for children to play near one another comfortably. Even infants like to watch what other children are doing. Here are some suggestions for toy arrangement.

Put out a few toys at a time. Too many toys can overwhelm young children. Change your inventory as children master each rotation of toys or get tired of them. However, do not remove all of the toys that children have mastered. As in familiar books, children find comfort in favorite toys.

Have duplicates of most toys. Children younger than age 3 have a difficult time sharing. You can minimize conflicts by providing duplicates.

Store toys on low shelves. If toys are stored on the bottom ledge of a bookcase or room divider, children can get them when they want to play with them. Leave ample space between stored toys to make it easy for the children to see each one. Avoid using toy chests. They are safety hazards, and it is difficult for children to find toys in them.

Make a label for each type of toy. Picture and word labels placed on containers and shelves show children where things belong. You can draw a picture of the toy, photograph it, or cut a picture of it from a catalog. This helps children find what they want, and cleaning up becomes a matching game.

Group similar toys together. This helps children locate their favorite puzzles, transportation toys, push-and-pull toys, and so forth. Grouping by type also helps teach children to classify objects.

Provide a protected area for block building. One option is to use a corner of the room with a shelf or couch to protect a space for builders. Children can play with soft blocks anywhere: on a rug, linoleum, or a wooden floor. Small table blocks can be used on a table or on the floor.

Caring and Teaching

It is fascinating to watch what infants, toddlers, and twos do with the toys and objects you provide. By observing purposefully, taking a real interest in what they do, and responding to them, you will learn much about what interests each child and appreciate what each child is doing and learning.

Young Infants

Very young infants are much more interested in watching your face, hearing your voice, and being held than in any toy. Once they can focus on objects better and hold them in their fists, they are ready to respond to the toys you provide.

> **Linda** has a soft play mat with an attached play gym. She lays Julio (4 months) on his back, and he reaches for the dangling toys, batting them with his hand. Linda talks to him as he plays. "You like the play gym, don't you, Julio? You're having a good time. You discovered that the toy moves when you hit it. Now you're watching it go back and forth, back and forth." Linda is careful to observe for cues that Julio is ready to do something else.

Just as an infant lets you know when he is hungry, tired, or in need of changing, his behavior lets you know when he is ready to play or when he is finished with one play experience and ready for another.

Here are the kinds of things Janet might say to Jasmine as they play together.

> **Jasmine** (8 months) can now sit by herself and scoot around on the floor, so Janet encourages her play by placing a mirror near the floor. When they play peek-a-boo, Jasmine can watch the action in the mirror.

- Describe the experience: *There's Jasmine, in the mirror.*
- Verbalize feelings: *That surprised you, didn't it?*
- Play with language: *Peek-a-boo. I see you. Peek-a, peek-a-BOO!*
- Describe actions: *You can see yourself in the mirror. There's Jasmine.*

Mobile Infants

Mobile infants seem to be in love with the world and fascinated by everything in it. They are immediately interested when you place a basket of toys near them and will proceed to pull out every object they can reach, dumping each on the floor and then reaching for another. Filling and dumping are favorite activities of this age-group. Any container and object (or objects) will work. They also enjoy tossing things, so give them plenty of space and soft, unbreakable toys.

> **Abby** (14 months) is playing with vinyl blocks. She attempts to stack them, but they keep falling over. Instead of building a tower for her as a model, Brooks works with Abby to help her figure out a solution. She encourages Abby to experiment with placing the cubes. Through trial and error, Abby eventually learns that the more fully the top cube covers the bottom one, the steadier the tower will be.

Take time to watch and think about what a child is experiencing and about how and when you might respond. Here is what you might say and do.

- Describe what the child does and what happens (cause and effect): *Look what happened when you pushed the button. The clown popped out!*

- Encourage the child to solve problems: *Oh, the ball rolled under the table. How can you get it?*

- Build vocabulary by using descriptive words: *You decided to play with the red fire truck. It's the same color as your red shirt.*

- Promote a recognition of group needs: *You put all of the blocks back in the bucket where we keep them. That was a big job, so you and* [another child] *did it together.*

Toddlers

Toddlers use toys with increasing intention. As they play, they build their physical and language skills, learn concepts, apply thinking skills, explore the world of social roles and make-believe, and learn to be a member of a group. Here are some ways to respond to their play.

- To promote physical skills: *I see that you are using your big muscles today. Thank you for helping me carry these big blocks over to the tree.*

- To support thinking skills: *Can you find the picture on the shelf that matches the snap beads?*

- Encourage perseverance: *It's hard to get that puzzle piece to fit. Why don't you turn it around and see if it fits then? I bet you can get it to fit.*

- Promote a recognition of the needs of others: *You are waiting patiently for your turn with the ride-on toy.*

Twos

It is fascinating to watch what twos do with toys. As long as you do not give them too many choices and you show an interest in what they are doing, their use of materials can be creative and joyful. Engage twos in conversation about what they want to play with and what they intend to do. In addition to the kinds of comments and descriptions explained earlier, invite twos to tell you what they are doing. Use open-ended questions to encourage them to think about what they are doing and to verbalize their thoughts. Here are some ways to interact with twos as they play with toys.

- Invite the child to talk about what he has done: *Tell me why you arranged the cars that way.*

- Describe what you see: *First you used all of the rectangular blocks to build your farm. Then you added animals, and now you are adding people.*

- Support social skills: *Why don't you both take the Bristle Blocks® over to the rug so you can play together?*

- Promote problem-solving skills: *When you put the big block on top of the little one, your building fell down. How can you build it so it won't fall?*

- Ask open-ended questions: *What do you think will happen if you try it another way?*

Responding to and Planning for Each Child

As you observe children playing with toys, think about the objectives for development and learning. Consider what each child is learning and how you might respond. Here is how four teachers who are implementing *The Creative Curriculum*® use what they learn from their observations to respond to each child and to plan.

Observe	Reflect	Respond
Julio (4 months) lies on his tummy on a play mat. He reaches for a teether, grabs it, and brings it to his mouth. He continues to look around the mat for several minutes, and then he notices two children pushing trucks. He watches them and begins to grunt, moving his head up and down.	Julio is using his whole hand to grasp objects (*Objective 6, Demonstrates gross-motor manipulative skills*). He is beginning to move purposefully (*Objective 4, Demonstrates traveling skills*). He watches and responds to other children (*Objective 2, Establishes and sustains positive relationships; Dimension c, Interacts with peers*).	Linda decides to encourage Julio's interest in the other children by responding to the cues that tell her that he would like to change his position. She says, "You see those two girls playing with the trucks. I'll pick you up, and we'll move closer so you can see them better."
Abby (14 months) fills a purse with small blocks and carries it as she toddles around the room. She approaches Samanda, opens the purse to show her what is inside, and then continues carrying it around.	Abby is walking with increasing coordination (*Objective 4, Demonstrates traveling skills*). She is engaging momentarily with other children (*Objective 2, Establishes and sustains positive relationships; Dimension c, Interacts with peers*).	Brooks provides other objects for Abby to carry, so Abby can strengthen her large-muscle skills and balance. She encourages her engagement with other children by saying, "Abby, I think Samanda wants to look carefully at the blocks you collected. Will you please show them to her again?"

Observe	Reflect	Respond
Leo (18 months) takes the top off a shape sorter and dumps out all of the shapes. He brings it over to a bucket of plastic people and begins to fill the sorter with the people. When the sorter is full and no more people will fit, he holds it up to Barbara and asks, "Mo'?"	Leo is using one hand to hold an object and the other hand to manipulate another object (*Objective 7, Demonstrates fine-motor strength and coordination; Dimension a, Uses fingers and hands*). He is experimenting with trial and error approaches to simple problems (*Objective 11, Demonstrates positive approaches to learning; Dimension c, Solves problems*). He is using gestures, word-like sounds, and single words to communicate (*Objective 9, Uses language to express thoughts and needs; Dimension b, Speaks clearly*).	Barbara responds to Leo by describing the problem: "I don't think any more will fit in there, Leo." She encourages him to solve the problem by asking, "What else can you put the people in?" She pauses, giving him time to think about the question, and then offers some suggestions. She asks, "How about using a bigger container so that more people will fit?" Then, as she points to a collection of baskets and a cardboard box, she adds, "We have baskets and a big box."
Gena (30 months) is playing with the farm animals. She puts three horses next to each other, places two pigs together, and matches two sheep. She looks up and says, "Same, same. All the same."	Gena is grouping objects with similar characteristics (*Objective 13, Uses classification skills*). She uses simple sentences with three or more words (*Objective 9, Uses language to express thoughts and needs; Dimension c, Uses conventional grammar*).	Ivan acknowledges Gena's work, saying, "I see you have put all the horses together, the pigs together, and the sheep together." To encourage her language development, he expands what she said. "All of the horses, all of the pigs, and all of the sheep. The same kind of animal goes together."

Responsive Planning

In developing weekly plans, these teachers use their observations and refer to *Objectives for Development & Learning*. This is what they record on their weekly planning forms.

- On the "Child Planning Form," under "Current information," Linda writes about the cues Julio used to tell her that he was ready to do something else. Under "Plans," she writes that she will observe Julio closely so that she can respond appropriately to his cues. She also writes a reminder to share what she learns with her co-teacher.

- After reviewing observation notes about the other children, Brooks realizes that two other children have been carrying toys in purses. She decides to add some small baskets for filling and carrying. Brooks adds this task to the "Group Planning Form" under "Changes to the Environment."

- Barbara recognizes that Leo was exploring the concept of quantity (how many he can fit into the container). On the "Child Planning Form," under "Plans," she records that she will provide opportunities for him to experiment with quantity through water play. On the "Group Planning Form," under "Changes to the Environment," she records, "Add 2 sets of nesting cups to the water table." She also makes a note to use words such as *more, less, same, empty,* and *full* with the children.

- Ivan uses the "Child Planning Form" to record his observation of Gena's expressive language. Under "Plans," he writes that he will continue to expand her sentences, offering her opportunities to hear more complex language and new words. He also decides to bring a collection of lids that he can put in small tubs for the children to sort. He adds this to the "Group Planning Form" under "Indoor Experiences" for Monday, Tuesday, and Wednesday.

Sharing Thoughts About the Value of Toys

Dear Families:

Toys are designed for children's enjoyment. They are also important tools for learning. When children play with toys, they learn how to move, how things work, and how to communicate with and relate to others. Here are just a few of the ways that toys help your child grow and learn.

When your child does this…	Your child is learning…
• bats a ball to make it move	• cause and effect
• rolls a toy car	• about movement and space
• puts pieces in a form board	• concepts such as shape, size, color
• snaps plastic beads together	• eye-hand coordination
• builds with blocks	• how objects can be used

What You Can Do at Home

Here are some ideas that can help your child make the most of playing with toys at home.

- **You are your child's favorite toy.** Your interest and involvement make playing with toys even more fun and engaging.

- **A few good toys are better than too many.** Too many toys can overwhelm a young child. It's far better to have a few good toys that can be used in a variety of ways.

- **Choose simple toys at first.** Good toys for infants are those that they can explore with all their senses. Plastic rings and rattles that they can grasp, squeeze, and mouth are especially good. Mobile infants enjoy playing with toys that they can push or pull, such as plastic lawn mowers. They also like toys with movable parts, such as doors, knobs, big buttons, switches, and so on.

- **Pick toys that challenge your child.** Toddlers are ready for simple puzzles with 4–5 pieces, plastic and wooden cars and trucks, blocks, shape sorters, nesting cups, and riding toys. Your 2-year-old will enjoy puzzles with more pieces, matching games, large beads and laces, balls, and blocks of all kinds.

- **Common household objects make wonderful toys.** An empty box, large empty thread spools, pots and pans, plastic food containers, and kitchen utensils are just a few of the things that young children use as toys.

Whether you buy or make your child's toys, what's most important is that you take pleasure in watching your child play, talk about what he or she is doing, and respond enthusiastically to each new discovery.

Sincerely,

Imitating and Pretending

Supporting Development and Learning 276

**Creating an Environment
for Pretend Play** 277
Selecting Materials for Different Ages 277
Setting Up and Displaying Materials 279

Caring and Teaching 280
Responding to and Planning for Each Child 284

**Sharing Thoughts About Imitation
and Pretend Play** 287

Imitating and Pretending

Leo (18 months) is sitting on the floor with a large pot and wooden spoon. "It looks like you are busy cooking something, Leo," remarks Barbara. Leo continues to stir. "What are you making?" she asks. Leo looks up and smiles. Barbara says, "M-m-m, it smells like pea soup to me." When Leo nods, Barbara says, "I thought so. May I please have some of your soup?" She gets a bowl and hands it to Leo. When he doesn't respond, Barbara says, "Oh, I'm silly. You need a big ladle to serve the soup." She hands a ladle to Leo, who pretends to serve some soup to her.

Pretending is a way of learning as well as a way of playing, and it requires a great deal of thinking. Pretending shows that children are developing from the sensorimotor thinking of infancy to more mature symbolic thinking. It evolves gradually from the imitation and exploration of infants, toddlers, and twos.

Young infants imitate facial expressions, many of the language sounds they hear, and the immediate actions of others. By about age 15 months, mobile infants can remember the actions on objects that they have previously seen others perform, so they are able to imitate those actions later.[39] Being able to remember and then imitate an action is important to early pretend play, which often takes the form of reproducing the actions children have seen others make. Toddlers and twos remember past experiences and often purposefully pretend to be something or someone else, such as a great big monster or a daddy feeding a baby.

When you show an infant how to wave bye-bye, clap her hands together, and play peek-a-boo, you are encouraging her to engage with others and to imitate speech and actions. When you see a mobile infant imitating a puppy and you say, "What a nice puppy!" you are encouraging him to continue to pretend. When you hold a doll on your shoulder and pat its back, you are showing a toddler how to pretend about real life situations. When you hand a toy phone to a 2-year-old so he can pretend to call the doctor about his sick baby, you are teaching him how to pretend with objects.

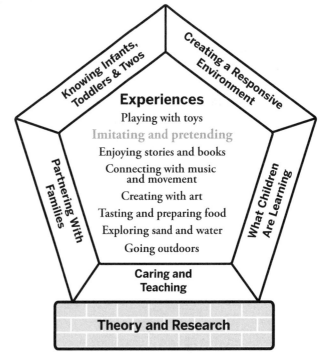

Supporting Development and Learning

Children develop social–emotional, physical, cognitive, and language skills when they imitate and pretend. Here are just a few examples.

Learning about self and others: Managing their feelings is one of the most important things that children under age 3 are learning. When they pretend to be a scary dog or an angry mother, they are experimenting with safe ways to express a range of feelings. They also explore emotions when they believe that dolls and stuffed animals have feelings and should be cared for.[40] As the brief play encounters of mobile infants with other children develop into coordinated play as children approach age 2, they begin to develop understandings about friendship. As twos assume pretend roles, you might observe them taking on the roles of important people in their lives by selecting particular items that represent those roles.

Learning about moving and doing: While they explore, imitate and pretend, very young children strengthen their large-muscle skills and refine their small-muscle skills. Perhaps they pretend to be a kitty cat that is crawling around a box or a father who runs to catch the bus. Maybe they push a doll carriage or a toy shopping cart full of empty food boxes. Such experiences involve large muscles. They practice using small muscles when they press the buttons on the toy phone, dress a doll, or put things in a suitcase or pocketbook.

Learning about the world: Young children use imitation to make sense of their experiences and to interact with others socially. As their physical skills mature and as they gain experience with the world, they begin to act out events and familiar routines. They also begin to explore social roles, especially those of parents and other powerful figures. In your simple pretend play area, children show that they know how objects can be used. The play stove is for pretending to cook, a doll bed is for pretending that a baby is sleeping. The fire hat prompts toddlers and twos to pretend to drive to a fire, first using a realistic steering wheel but later pretending to drive just by turning their hands in space to indicate the motion of a turning steering wheel.

Learning about communicating: As you wave good-bye to a baby's father early in the morning, you say, "Bye-bye, Daddy." Up goes the baby's hand, opening and shutting, imitating your farewell gesture. Gestures and, later, words continue during games of peek-a-boo, as you and the infant pretend to disappear and, to the baby's glee, reappear in a delightful two-way conversation of sorts that encourages children to engage in play. Single words, two-word phrases, and simple sentences appear in pretend play as infants become toddlers and toddlers become twos. "Baby hungry," a toddler says as he feeds a baby doll. A 2-year-old might explain, "My baby likes 'nanas."

Creating an Environment for Pretend Play

A few well-chosen props and materials invite infants, toddlers, and twos to imitate and pretend. As they get older, additional realistic props inspire twos to take on different roles and pretend about situations they have experienced.

Selecting Materials for Different Ages

Young Infants

Materials that allow young infants to use all of their senses and that promote their physical skills are appropriate, such as soft dolls or stuffed animals that they can grasp and hold. Dolls should be washable and have simple facial features with no moveable pieces or detachable parts. Young infants especially like bright colors and objects that have rattles inside and make noise when shaken. Offer play items that allow them to try different actions and to watch what happens as a result.

Your daily interactions are as important as the toys and other items you provide. Babies prefer to play when they are with nurturing adults. As they experiment with toys and other objects, young infants imitate the actions of other people and try new ways to make things happen.

Mobile Infants

These active explorers like to push; pull; shake; bang; fill and dump; and climb in, out, around, and on top of furniture and equipment. Realistic toys are good choices for mobile infants. They respond to lifelike dolls of vinyl or rubber that they can carry, hold, and pretend to feed. Here are suggestions of popular materials:

- carts, baby carriages, and other wheeled toys
- doll bottles, baby blankets, and a cradle
- toy or real telephones
- hats and pocketbooks
- pots, pans, and plastic dishes and utensils
- plastic, wood, or rubber cars, buses, trucks, planes, and trains

Notice what happens when you put out realistic toys and objects. See if a mobile infant picks up a cup and pretends to drink or places a doll in a toy stroller and pushes it around the room.

Toddlers and Twos

Because they take great interest in the details of toys and props, toddlers and twos are intrigued by small cars with doors that open and shut; trucks with movable parts; and dolls with movable arms and legs, hair, and facial features. Provide props that encourage role playing, especially the roles of parents and other powerful figures such as monsters, doctors, and firefighters. Props such as toy household items also encourage children to replay parts of their everyday experiences. Dolls should represent the ethnicities of the children in your program.

As older toddlers and twos develop more small-muscle control, it is possible for them to handle simple doll clothes and dress-up clothes. They might play for long periods of time, for example, arranging people and animal figures in- and outside of a toy barn and talking to them as they play. By regularly rotating the props you make available, you can keep toddlers and twos interested and extend their play.

In addition to the materials listed for mobile infants, consider adding these materials:

- dress-up clothes, such as jackets, hats, and dresses
- work-related props, such as boots, firefighter hats, work gloves, stethoscopes
- suitcases, pocketbooks, and lunch boxes
- doll bottles, baby blankets, and a cradle or small box to serve as a doll bed
- child-size dishes, pots, and pans
- child-size broom and mop
- assorted plastic containers and empty food boxes

For 2-year-olds, prop boxes are a good way to organize a collection of items related to a particular pretend play theme. For example, they may replay firsthand experiences at the doctor's office when they open a hospital prop box containing materials such as these:

- white or green shirts or old scrubs, and nurses caps
- stethoscope
- gauze and adhesive bandages
- pads and markers for prescriptions
- toy syringe

Similarly, a supermarket prop box might contain empty food containers, paper bags, and plastic fruits and vegetables. Think about experiences the children have had and what props might spark their interest and encourage them to pretend.

Setting Up and Displaying Materials

While infants do not need to have an area set aside for imitating, toddlers and especially twos will be drawn to an area arranged for pretend play. In a defined area, you can display the objects and props you know children will enjoy. Because they are most likely to pretend about their own lives, a simple house corner is ideal. A small table and chairs, a doll bed, a carriage, and a sink and stove create a place for toddlers and twos to engage in pretend play.

Place picture and word labels of the items where the materials are stored, so children learn where to find what they need and where to return it when they finish playing. An orderly arrangement of the materials conveys the message that you want children to use the materials and take care of them. Here are some ideas for storing and displaying props and materials:

- Use wooden pegs on a board to hang clothes, hats, and pocketbooks.

- Store shoes and other small items in a shoe bag.

- Hang dress-up clothes on a small coat tree that has been shortened to the children's level.

- Suspend three-tiered wire baskets from a hook to hold plastic food, ties and scarves, costume jewelry, and doll clothes.

- Hang pots, pans, cooking utensils, mops, brooms, and dress-up clothes on a pegboard with hooks.

Avoid displaying too many things at once. Too many choices overwhelm children, and they stop playing. Keep in mind that, while props can be very helpful in extending pretend play, the best way to encourage this type of play is to show your interest in what children do and follow their lead in pretending. Imitating and pretending with young children is another opportunity to build relationships that enable children to thrive.

Caring and Teaching

By observing children carefully, by taking a real interest and delight in what they do, and by playing games and having fun with children, you help them learn how to play and how to interact with other children. You also help them learn through their play. *Objectives for Development & Learning* will help you determine each child's developmental level for particular objectives. The information will help you decide what each child needs from you and how best to respond in ways that support each child's developing abilities.

Young Infants

Your relationship with young infants builds the foundation for all learning, including their ability to gain the most from imitation and play. Secure relationships make it easier for children to interact with other people, and they encourage children to play. Children's explorations become increasingly purposeful over time.

> **Julio** (4 months) grasps a doll and immediately puts it into his mouth. **Jasmine** (8 months) has more ways of exploring. She may turn the doll over to examine it from different angles and then pat it gently.

As early as 2 months of age, babies are fascinated by each other. They get excited when they see other infants, and they stare at each other when they have chances to do so.[41] If you work with 6- to 9-month-old infants, notice how they try to get and return the attention of other children by smiling and babbling. Offer safe opportunities for young infants to be together, and encourage their interest in what other children are doing.

As you care for young infants, take time to talk with them about ways they are imitating and socializing. Here are some examples:

- Repeat the language sounds a child makes: *I hear you saying, "Ba-ba-ba." Now I'm going to say it: "Ba-ba-ba." Can you do that again?*

- Describe what a child is doing: *You like watching the other children. I see you smiling at them.*

- Engage a child in repeating actions in a fingerplay: *You clapped your hands together! Let's do it again. Pat-a-cake, pat-a cake, baker's man.*

Mobile Infants

Your playfulness and the various materials you provide become increasingly important as infants become more mobile. At this stage, infants explore objects and find out what they can do with them, sometimes by exploring new ways but often by imitating what they have previously seen others do with them. By about 10 months, an infant's brief action shows that she understands how an object is used, but she is not yet pretending. For example, she brings an empty spoon to her mouth while you are feeding her. Later, a mobile infant shows an awareness of pretending during an activity that only involves himself, as when he closes his eyes tightly and laughs while pretending to sleep.[42]

As they get older, you might observe mobile infants amusing themselves by playing with materials in unconventional ways.

> **Willard** (11 months) takes a hat, puts it on his foot, and looks at Grace with an impish grin. To participate in the game, Grace shakes her head, smiles, and says, "No-o-o, not there! A hat doesn't go on your foot." Willard continues the game, putting the hat on different parts of his body and waiting to see Grace's reaction. He finally puts it on his head and he laughs when she confirms, "That's right. A hat goes on your head!"

As much as mobile infants enjoy playing with you, they are also becoming quite interested in each other. By 9–12 months, they imitate and touch each other. They handle objects together and may play for longer periods. During the next six months, children begin to exchange roles in action games, such as taking turns chasing and being chased. When they have the opportunity to play with familiar peers, children tend to engage in the same kinds of play. Even at this young age, children seem to understand when another person wants to play and what the person wants to do.[43]

Mobile infants are fascinating to watch. Take time to observe what they do and think about what you are learning before you decide how to respond. When you describe what children are doing and ask questions, you help them become aware of their actions. Here are some examples:

- Sing songs and fingerplays that involve simple actions: *Let's sing "The Wheels on the Bus." Can you make your hands go 'round and 'round?*

- Respond to a child who is pretending to be a dog: *Hello little puppy dog. Why are you barking? Are you hungry? Here's a bone for you"*

- Provide multiples of pretend play props, to minimize waiting and conflicts: *Here is another pot so you can make lunch, too.*

Toddlers

The pretend play of toddlers is more complex. Either their play involves another person or object, such as a stuffed animal, or the child acts out an activity that they have seen performed by someone else.[44] They enact simple routines, using objects in play as they are used in real life, such as combing a doll's hair or feeding a doll a bottle. Later they begin to substitute one object for another while they pretend, such as using a ring from a stacking toy as a bagel or a cylindrical block as a baby bottle to feed a doll. You will notice that children use objects that resemble in size and shape the ones they represent.

As toddlers learn more about the world, they typically develop fears about such things as loud noises, large animals, being separated from their families, and going to the doctor. Pretend play is one way that they cope with their fears.

> **Leo** (18 months) stamps around the room, growling and swiping the air with his arms. He is assuming the role of the scary monster he most fears. By becoming the monster, he can control what the monster does and thereby experience some power over what he fears. Barbara responds, "Oh, my, what a scary monster! I bet that monster is looking for a friend. I'll be your friend, Mr. Monster. Come play with me."

By accepting this type of play, verbalizing what you think a child is feeling, and joining in, you can help toddlers work through fears that they cannot express directly. For this reason, pretend play is as important to a child's emotional development as it is to cognitive and social development.

Take time to encourage children's interest in pretending. You can do this by talking about what they are doing and by joining their play. Here are some examples:

- Provide props: *Here are some empty food boxes to put in your shopping cart.*
- Pretend along with toddlers: *Will you please take me for a ride in your car?*
- Describe what a child is doing: *I see that you are taking the baby for a ride in the carriage. Are you taking her to the park?*

Twos

The play of 2-year-olds becomes increasingly social and complex. At first, they share a common play theme without combining their activities with each other. For example, they might both pretend to make lunch, but each will pretend to pour milk instead of one child's pretending to serve the other. By about age 30 months, children begin to assume roles that go with another child's role, such as pretending to be a parent when the other child is pretending to be a baby.[45]

Sometimes children get so immersed in their play, you might have difficulty getting their attention for another purpose. Play is also a child's private reality at that moment,[46] so a child who has assumed the role of someone else might correct you when you call her by her given name.

> **Gena** (30 months) tells Ivan, "I not Gena. I Pooh Bear." Ivan plays along, "Okay, Pooh. It's time to eat your honey."

Twos are beginning to plan their play. They reenact events and announce what they are going to do. They also combine a sequence of tasks while they pretend.[47] For example, Jonisha may gather together several items needed to "play baby," and then hold the doll, pretend to feed it, and put it to bed. Two children might put on firefighter hats and pretend to put out a fire together. They may pretend with objects that do not closely resemble what they represent, such as by picking up a piece of string, pretending that it is a hose and using it to squirt imaginary water on an imaginary fire. This is an important achievement and shows that they are able to imagine a hose, fire, and water without relying on realistic props. Their increasing ability to use language to communicate with each other also makes their play more complex and interesting, and it helps them keep their play going.

When twos engage in this type of pretend play, encourage them by providing the materials they need, talking with them, and participating in the play. Here are some examples:

- Provide props to extend children's interests: *Did the car break down? Uh, oh! We'd better get the tool box and see what we can do to fix it.*

- Describe what a child is doing: *I see that you are wearing the firefighter hat and that you have a hose. Is a house on fire?*

- Participate in pretend play by taking on a role: *Hello? Hello? Is this the doctor? I have a sick baby here. We need to see the doctor. Is she in the office today?*

- Encourage a child to pretend without props: As you hand the child an imaginary phone, say, *The doctor wants to talk to you.*

- Ask open-ended questions to encourage imaginative thinking and expressive language: *I see you have packed your suitcase. Where are you going? How will you get there?*

Young children engaged in pretend play have many ideas and are often very imaginative. Take time to observe and appreciate what they are doing. Then take on a role, yourself; join them in their pretend play; and help them interact with other children. Always match the child's pace, recognizing that some children—because of a disability, temperament, or inexperience— may respond more slowly or need more support from you.

Responding to and Planning for Each Child

As you observe children imitating and pretending, think about the objectives for development and learning. Consider what each child is learning and how you should respond. Here is how four teachers who are implementing *The Creative Curriculum®* use what they learn from their observations to respond to each child and to plan.

Observe	Reflect	Respond
Jasmine (8 months) picks up a bright red plastic block and examines it. She looks at Holly, who is banging a wooden spoon on an empty oatmeal box. After watching her, Jasmine starts to bang her block on the floor.	Jasmine is watching and responding to other children (*Objective 2, Establishes and sustains positive relationships*; *Dimension c, Interacts with peers*). She imitates the actions of others (*Objective 14, Uses symbols and images to represent something not present*; *Dimension b, Engages in sociodramatic play*).	Janet describes what Jasmine is doing, "You are watching Holly and making a big noise by banging that block. She imitates Jasmine's actions, using a cup: "I think I'll see what noise I can make with this cup. Bang, bang."
Abby (14 months) goes over to Jessie (16 months), who is wearing a hat, and tries to take it off. Brooks says, "Jessie is wearing that hat. I see you want one, too." She hands Abby a hat. Abby accepts it, puts it on her head, and smiles at Jessie.	Abby responds to verbal redirection (*Objective 1, Regulates own emotions and behaviors*; *Dimension b, Follows limits and expectations*). She has brief play encounters with other children (*Objective 2, Establishes and sustains positive relationships*; *Dimension c, Interacts with peers*).	Brooks wants to encourage Abby's interest in other children. She tries to involve her in pretending with one or two other children. She says, "Now you each have a hat to wear. Would you like to play with these trucks while you wear your hats?"
Matthew (22 months) is wearing a firefighter hat and holding a paper towel roll. He walks around the room saying, "Shhhh. Out, fire!"	Matthew substitutes one object for another in pretend play (*Objective 14, Uses symbols and images to represent something not present*; *Dimension b, Engages in sociodramatic play*). He is beginning to express himself in two-word phrases (*Objective 9, Uses language to express thoughts and needs*; *Dimension c, Uses conventional grammar*).	Mercedes expands what Matthew says and asks questions to encourage him to express his ideas verbally and extend his pretend play: "I see you have a hose to squirt the fire. Is it a big fire? Do you need a lot of water? Here, I'll turn on the fire hydrant for you. Is that enough water?"

Observe	Reflect	Respond
Valisha (33 months) puts a plastic stethoscope around her neck and announces, "Doctor is here." Jonisha (33 months) holds up a baby doll and explains, "She sick. She needs some medicine." Valisha says, "Okay," as she opens the black bag she is holding. "Here's some," she says as she hands Jonisha a small wooden block.	Valisha and Jonisha are using objects in pretend play as they are used in real life and substituting one object for another in pretend play (*Objective 14, Uses symbols and images to represent something not present*; *Dimension b, Engages in sociodramatic play*). They are participating in coordinated play (*Objective 9, Establishes and sustains positive relationships*; *Dimension c, Interacts with peers*). They are using simple sentences with three or more words (*Objective 9, Uses language to express thoughts and needs*; *Dimension c, Uses conventional grammar*).	Deciding not to interrupt their play, LaToya observes the sisters as they continue to play with the doctor props and doll. She pulls a piece of paper out of her pocket and writes a quick observation note describing their pretend play.

Responsive Planning

In developing weekly plans, these teachers use their observations and refer to *Objectives for Development & Learning*. This is what they record on their weekly planning forms.

- On the "Child Planning Form," under "Current Information," Janet writes that Jasmine is beginning to imitate the actions of others. Under "Plans," she writes that she will involve Jasmine in some new fingerplays and encourage her to imitate the actions. On the "Group Planning Form", Janet lists the new fingerplays and songs she wants to introduce to the children.

- Brooks makes a note on the "Child Planning Form," under "Current Information," that Abby is showing an interest in other children. She wants to encourage this, so, under "Plans," she records that she will invite Abby and Jessie to help her make playdough. On the "Group Planning Form," she writes that she will make playdough with the children on Monday.

- On the "Child Planning Form," under "Current Information," Mercedes documents Matthew's interest in firefighters and his ability to pretend. She decides that this is something she wants to encourage. In the "Changes to the Environment" section of her "Group Planning Form," Mercedes writes that she will add firefighter boots and rain slickers to the dramatic play area, fire trucks in the block area, and some storybooks and nonfiction books in the library.

- On the "Child Planning Form," under "Current Information," LaToya notes that Jonisha and Valisha are acting out more complex pretend play scenarios. Because the group is going to take a walk to a local veterinary hospital next week, LaToya decides that she will add some stuffed animals and blank prescription pads to the doctor props. She records this idea under "Plans." She then lists the prescription pads and the animals she will add on the "Group Planning Form," under "Changes to the Environment."

Infants, toddlers, and twos engage in imitation and pretend play when they are encouraged by the adults they love. Your ongoing observations of children will enable you to respond to them intentionally and use what you learn to plan experiences that will support their development and learning. Families also play a key role in supporting this type of play. They will be more likely to engage in imitation and pretend play with their children if they understand the importance of play. The letter to families is one way to share this information.

Dear Families:

Imitation and pretend play are among the most important ways that children learn about the world and relationships with people. The foundation for this type of play begins when young infants form secure attachments with the important people in their lives and explore their surroundings. They imitate other people, in order to understand how objects are used and as a way to get and keep the attention of others. Before long, they make believe with realistic items. For example, a toddler might feed a doll with a spoon or rock a doll to sleep. Two-year-olds learn to use objects to stand for other things, for example, to use a block as a car by pushing it along the floor.

As social pretend play begins, children explore social roles such as being a mother, a father, a doctor, and a baby. Being able to pretend also helps children cope with fears and anxieties. This is why children pretend to go to the doctor or to be a monster. Children who have good pretend play skills are more likely to be ready for school than those who lack these skills, because pretend play benefits every aspect of a young child's development. Children who have good pretend play skills are also often good at making friends.

What You Can Do at Home

Because imitation and pretend play are so important to every child's development and eventual success in school, we hope you will pretend with your child at home.

- **Encourage your child to explore.** The more children learn about objects and people, the more information they have on which to base their pretend play.

- **Talk about real life experiences as they take place.** When you take your child to various places—to the grocery store, post office, or a clinic—talk about what is happening. Explain what people are doing, their jobs, and the names of tools and other objects they use. This helps your child understand and recall experiences.

- **Provide props that inspire pretend play.** Dolls, doll blankets, a cradle, telephones (toy or real), pots, pans, and plastic dishes will inspire your child to explore social roles. Other useful props include plastic people and animals; transportation toys such as cars, trucks, and boats; and various ride-on toys.

- **Let your child dress up.** You can encourage your child's interest in pretending by providing dress-up clothes and work-related props such as firefighter hats, work gloves, and a toy stethoscope.

- **Play make-believe with your child.** This is one of the best ways to encourage your child to pretend. You can also encourage pretend play by asking questions; offering a new prop; and taking on a role, yourself.

Together we can help your child use imitation and pretend play as important ways to learn.

Sincerely,

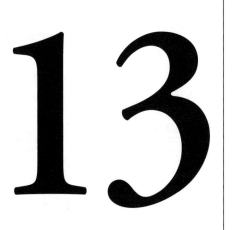

13

Enjoying Stories and Books

Supporting Development and Learning 290

**Creating an Environment for
Enjoying Stories and Books   291**
Selecting Books for Different Ages   291
Setting Up and Displaying Materials   295

Caring and Teaching   296
Including All Children   300
Responding to and Planning for Each Child   302

**Sharing Thoughts About
Enjoying Stories and Books   305**

Enjoying Stories and Books

Matthew (24 months) hands Mercedes a book as they sit together in the book area. She asks, "Do you want me to read Mrs. Wishy-Washy *again?" Matthew opens the book to the picture of the cow in the tub. "In went the cow," says Mercedes. "Wishy-washy, wishy-washy," Matthew responds. "In went the pig," Mercedes reads. "Wishy-washy, wishy-washy," chant Marcella and Deneitra, who have joined them. "Away went the cow. Away went the pig. Away went the duck. Oh, lovely mud," Mercedes reads.[48] "Again, again," Matthew urges. "Love mud."*

Sharing stories and books with young children can be among the most treasured times of your day. With so many excellent books to touch, look at, and listen to, children will grow to love books. Even young infants, who do not yet understand the messages found in books, learn from exploring them.

Your interaction as you snuggle together with a book, your enthusiasm, the way you bring a story to life through your dramatic reading, and your interesting questions make the experience special for very young children. Because you know the children in your group so well, you can choose wonderful books for an infant to manipulate and explore, a toddler who is about to acquire a new brother or sister, or a 2-year-old who loves animals.

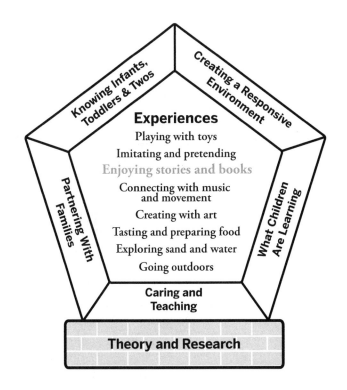

Supporting Development and Learning

Sharing stories and books with infants, toddlers, and twos supports their development and learning in many ways. Here are just a few examples.

Learning about themselves and others: The comfort of a favorite teacher's lap and the warmth of her voice create enjoyable associations with books and reading. Well before they understand the words, children gain a sense of security from the familiar rhythm of a favorite sleep-time book. As children grow older, they begin to relate to pictures and stories of familiar places and events. Books help children learn about how people are the same and different. They help infants, toddlers, and twos to identify and handle their emotions, and to feel connected to their families throughout the day.

Learning about moving: Looking at books encourages very young children to use their fine-motor skills. Infants explore books in the same ways that they explore everything else. They reach for and grab, mouth and chew, shake, turn, and toss books. At 4–6 months, infants learn to grasp objects, including books. Sitting up frees a baby's hands to reach, grasp, and hold books. Mobile infants love to stick their fingers between pages, wave books in the air, point to pictures, and pat the illustrations. Toddlers can hold books with both hands and turn sturdy pages. Twos can turn the book right side up and carefully turn book pages without tearing them, most of the time.

Learning about the world: Books help children make sense of the world and learn new concepts. As they explore the properties of books, children learn about *light–heavy, big–little,* and *soft–hard*. As they look at picture books, they also learn concepts about size, number, and spatial relationships such as *up–down, in–out,* and *over–under*. Young children get information and learn how to do many things from books.

Learning about communicating: Storytelling and book reading help children build vocabulary and increasingly complex language skills. They enable young children to learn new words for naming animals, objects, actions, experiences, feelings, and ideas. A young infant enjoys the sounds of language as you read simple books. As you point to a picture of a cow, a mobile infant says, "Moo, moo," repeating the sounds you just made. Later, toddlers and twos name pictures and fill in repetitive words and phrases when you pause during readings. They explore book reading when they pretend to read to their dolls or tell their teddy bears a bedtime story.

Creating an Environment for Enjoying Stories and Books

Books must be a regular part of your program. All you need are books and comfortable places for children to look at them—on their own and with you—and to hear them read aloud. Looking at books is something children can do anywhere in your program. Encourage them to look at books on the floor, on their cots, and in a shady area outdoors.

Have soft, welcoming places for reading near the book display. An overstuffed cushion, covered mattress, carpeted risers, or a glider make book nooks cozy. Your space should be appropriate for reading with a small group of children as well as with one child at a time. Provide an inviting area where a toddler or 2-year-old can sink into a cushion or rock on a child-size rocker to look at a book by himself. Be prepared for the fact that the children's favorite books will migrate around the room, carried by mobile infants or brought to you by toddlers or twos.

Selecting Books for Different Ages

Select high-quality books that you will enjoy sharing with the children. Keep the children's developmental abilities in mind and look for books that respect diversity and promote inclusion. Rotate and add new books to encourage children's interest, but keep old favorites available for repeated (and repeated and repeated) readings.

Include some homemade books, especially for older toddlers and twos who love to see pictures and hear stories about themselves. You can pull out a book with family pictures when a child feels sad about saying good-bye to his mother. You can help children remember the first snowy day with pictures of them when they were frolicking in snowsuits and building a snowman. Digital cameras are a wonderful tool to make bookmaking easier. You can also make "feely" books with fabrics of different textures or with other familiar objects.

A visit to the children's room of your local library can help you supplement your program's book collection, as can organizations such as Reading Is Fundamental. Yard sales and thrift stores are good sources for inexpensive books to expand your collection and replace worn books.

Young Infants

Simple, bold illustrations interest young infants. As babies begin to reach and grasp, they become more active partners in reading. For the 4- to 6-month-old child, "reading" is sometimes book chewing, shaking, banging, sniffing, and observing. Older infants enjoy turning pages. Books for infants should focus on familiar things: bottles and food, clothes, toys, pets, and people. Stories should be simple, rhythmic, and sometimes wordless.

Good Books for Young Infants

- Washable, sturdy, chewable books made of cloth, plastic, or vinyl

- Board books that are easily cleaned, with pages that are easy to turn

- Books with highly contrasting pictures, or simple illustrations or photos, with one or two objects per page

- Books that have things to feel and move, such as tabs, flaps, holes, and a variety of textures

Mobile Infants

Recognizable pictures interest mobile infants. They begin to select books on the basis of content. They also enjoy books with repetition, rhyming verses, and nonsense syllables.

Good Books for Mobile Infants

- Sturdy books, such as board books

- Books with simple stories about babies, families, animals, and everyday experiences

- Books of songs, rhymes, and chants

- Simple stories with repetitive language

- Books with illustrations of familiar things that infants can point to or name

- Wordless books that picture familiar objects to name and count

Toddlers

Toddlers are beginning to follow simple plots. They especially like to hear stories about children and animals whose daily lives are similar to their own. Toddlers identify easily with mice who have grandmothers and with children who learn to use the potty.

This age-group enjoys the whole process of listening to a story read aloud. They like books with pages they can turn, illustrations they can point to as you ask questions, and phrases that sound silly and are repeated predictably.

Good Books for Toddlers

- Books that have simple plots and few words on each page

- Books about families and feelings, animals, and other everyday experiences such as saying *hello, good-bye,* and *goodnight*

- Books with pictures that introduce basic concepts about size, shape, and color

- Books where the words and related illustrations are placed closely together on the page

- Wordless books

- Alphabet books with simple, colorful illustrations

- Favorite stories, songs, or fingerplays that they can join in telling or acting out, such as "The Itsy Bitsy Spider"

- Books that make them laugh

- Books that encourage toddlers to hunt for and point to hidden objects

Twos

By the time they are age 2, children who have frequently heard books read aloud bring favorite books to you again and again. They are ready to complete the rhyme or fill in the word you omit as you read a familiar story to them. They may begin "reading" to you, a friend, or a doll by telling parts of a familiar story. Many twos will listen to a whole story, following the simple plot. They participate in book-related experiences, such as seeing what they can spy after listening to *Each Peach Pear Plum*, by Janet and Allen Ahlberg.

Good Books for Twos

- Stories about themselves or children who are like themselves

- Books about animals

- Stories they can join in telling or act out, such as Eric Carle's *From Head to Toe*

- Books with rhymes, songs and chants, and other predictable language patterns

- Book versions of familiar songs such as "Old McDonald"; "This Old Man"; or "Row, Row, Row Your Boat"

- Books that show human diversity

- Books that help children think and talk about their own lives because they relate to the children's experiences, such as learning personal care skills, or to the children's fears, such as anxiety about separation, getting lost, or making a mistake

- Alphabet books with simple, familiar themes

- Books that have pictures with details that provide information about the characters and their activities

- Books that help children understand concepts about number, size, shape, and color

Setting Up and Displaying Materials

One effective way to display books for toddlers and twos is in wall pockets made of heavy-duty fabric and clear vinyl. A book pocket looks like a shoe bag with one pocket for each book. The clear pockets protect the books while allowing children to see the covers. You can buy book pockets or make them yourself. For mobile infants to be able to get and handle the books, remove them from the pockets and stand them on a low table or on the floor. Thick cardboard books are best.

While book pockets can also be used with older infants and younger toddlers, you may prefer to display books by simply fanning them out on low, open shelves. This arrangement allows children to identify and reach for their favorites. A freestanding display encourages children to pick up a book whenever they are interested. Low shelves and baskets are also good ways to display books. The key is to display books so children can see and reach them.

Put out just a few books at the beginning of the year, but have a minimum of two books per child. Add more books as children develop book-handling skills. Rotate books regularly so that children are excited by new books, but remember to keep old favorites available to the children.

Display books in different places in your room for twos. For example, add books about families to the pretend play area and place books about buildings, farms, trucks, and animals near the blocks. Take books outdoors for reading in a shady, comfortable outdoor spot. Add other interesting props and materials that help support early literacy. Writing tools and paper encourage early scribbling. Include play props that encourage story telling and retelling, such as puppets and felt board pieces. For example, the children can arrange the three bears by size or match felt cutouts to those in Charles G. Shaw's *It Looked Like Spilt Milk*.

Wear and tear on books is inevitable with very young children. Do not let that stop you from making books available. While you expect wear and tear, always model treating books with care. Only display books that are in good repair. Torn books give the message that it is all right to tear books; books in good condition show that we take care of books. Repair torn books before returning them to the bookshelf.

Caring and Teaching

Relationships are at the heart of language and literacy learning. Exploring books and telling stories can be a cozy daily ritual and a way to calm an upset child. Make sure you read to every child, every day, either individually or in a shared reading experience. Reading aloud is one of the best ways to help children become successful readers.

Here are some general tips for reading and storytelling with children.

Become familiar with the book before you read it to the children. Think about what words might be new to the children so you can introduce them. Also think of questions you might ask about the pictures or the story.

Tell stories, as well as read them. The first time you read a story, talk or tell the story, rather than read it word for word. You can also tell stories by using wordless books and other storytelling props.

Make reading interactive. Set the stage. Snuggle. Build anticipation and excitement. Be a dramatic story reader, such as by pitching your voice high for Mama Bear and low for Papa Bear. Involve children in telling the story. Comment and wait for children to respond, ask questions and wait, and offer other prompts. Let children skip to their favorite pictures or pages. Encourage them to chant a book's repetitive phrases or fill in a missing rhyme. Point out when the story has ended, and ask whether they liked the story and whether they want to hear it again.

Follow the child's lead. Be ready to stop when the child loses interest. Watch for infants' cues. When young infants squirm, turn their head away, or push the book away, they are telling you that it is time to stop for now. Do not require children to sit during story time. While you are reading, allow children to crawl, toddle, or walk away and then return.

Be prepared to read the same story again and again. Children have favorites and do not tire of hearing those stories every day.

Link books to the daily routines in a child's life. If you are having difficulty calming a child for a nap, you might recite goodnight messages to some of the objects in your environment, just as in Margaret Wise Brown's *Goodnight Moon*. If you want to encourage children to dress themselves, you might repeat the advice given in Shigo Watanabe's *How Do I Put It On?*.

Provide opportunities for children to share books. One child can read to another or to a doll or puppet. As they develop understandings about stories and books, children retell stories they have heard many times or make up stories based on book illustrations.

Take advantage of storytelling and book reading opportunities as they occur. This can happen, for example, when a child brings you a book to read or comes to listen to a book you are reading with another child.

Extend the children's learning. For example, *Build It Up and Knock It Down* is a book by Tom Hunter, based on the song of the same name. Once you have read the book, you can listen to the song on a compact disc and the older children can sing along. They can act it out, play an opposites game, practice building and knocking down block buildings, and crawl in and out of large boxes that you have added to the indoor gross-motor area.

Young Infants

Sitting closely with you makes story and book experiences enjoyable for young infants. Choose a time when the baby is alert and well rested. Find a comfortable position for both you and the baby, perhaps with the baby snuggled on your lap or lying on the floor next to you. Read only a couple of pages and let the child turn the pages if he can. Read books the baby loves again and again.

Here are some more tips for enjoying stories and books with young infants:

- Offer a toy for a child to hold and chew while you read: *Here's a cuddly bear, just like the brown bear in the book.*

- Focus the child's attention by pointing to and naming things in the picture: *There's the baby's nose, and here's your nose!*

- Follow the child's lead: *You like the way that feels. It's soft and fuzzy.*

Mobile Infants

It is exciting when mobile infants recognize and point to pictures in books. They can listen for longer periods as you read very simple stories. You can even try reading to a group of two or three children. These experiences will be successful as long as you have realistic expectations of the children. Be prepared to stop at any point. Lost interest is your cue that the reading activity needs to be concluded. You can pick up the book again when a child shows interest.

Here are some tips for enjoying stories and books with mobile infants:

- Get the children's attention before starting: *Let's look at this book together.*
- Encourage the children to examine the illustrations as you read the text: *Can you find Spot in the picture? Point to the dog.*
- Take cues from the children's gestures, sounds, or words: *Yes, that is a baby, just like you.*
- Ask simple questions to help children understand what is being read, even if they cannot express themselves verbally yet: *They're going bye-bye, aren't they? Can you wave bye-bye like the mommy in the story?*

Toddlers

Reading with toddlers is much more interactive.

> **Matthew** (22 months) recites simple phrases from books that his parents and Mercedes have read and reread to him. If children are responsive, try reading a simple book all the way through. Toddlers can become caught up in the rhythm of the words and the flow of the plot. You will soon learn which books capture the children's attention and which children are ready to listen to an entire story.

Here are some tips for enjoying stories and books with toddlers:

- Pause during your reading and allow children time to anticipate the next words: The child choruses, "E-I-E-I-O," as you read *Old McDonald*.
- Respond to the children's verbal and nonverbal cues about the illustrations: *You're pointing to the dump truck. I know that you like big trucks.*
- Relate the story to the children's own lives: *You have a dog, just like the boy in the story.*

Twos

When they have had many chances to explore stories and books during their first two years, children 24–36 months begin to understand that there are different kinds of books. They also have definite favorites. Some books remind them of the things they do every day or of special events in their lives. Some tell stories about things that are not real. Help twos increase their vocabularies by reading books that have more extensive vocabularies than the children's speaking vocabularies. Read books that introduce new concepts through pictures and simple language.

Most twos can sit and be part of a small group of 2–4 children during a more formal, but brief, story time. Remember to let children decide how long they want to stay with the group.

Books with word play or refrains are especially good for small-group reading. You can help twos enjoy books by reading stories in ways that engage their emerging sense of humor. Skip an expected phrase or part of a familiar story from time to time. Switch words or play with words in silly ways. Twos love correcting you and making you read the story right, shouting out a predictable response together, or hearing how silly a funny word sounds when everyone says it at the same time.

While reading books with twos, try these tips:

- Set the stage for story reading by talking about the book cover: The Snowy Day, *by Eric Carle. What do you see in this picture?*

- Help them focus their attention and begin to predict the story: *Poor Corduroy lost his button. I wonder where it is.*

- Encourage children to use the illustrations to understand and explain what is going on and to make predictions: *Where are the children now? What do you think will happen to the little girl now that it is raining?*

- After reading the story through once, ask questions while you read it again: *Do you remember what the caterpillar eats next?*

Including All Children

By making some simple adaptations, you can make sure that all children—including dual language learners and children with disabilities—have enjoyable experiences with stories and books. The following suggestions help make stories and books meaningful for all children.

Dual-Language Learners

You can support children who are learning two languages by including, when possible, books and recorded readings in the children's home languages. Invite families to help you find stories to tell or read to the children. Families can also help you make homemade books and recordings. Make sure your collection includes books without words so children can look at pictures and name objects or talk about the pictures in their home languages and in English.

Story reading is an excellent way to help children who are learning English build both receptive and expressive language. Here are some useful techniques.

Read the story in the child's home language before reading it in English, if possible. Perhaps family members can read books in their home language.

Introduce key words and phrases in English and demonstrate the meaning with gestures or larger actions.

Use pictures, props, and other visual cues to help children understand the text. Point out details of the illustrations before you read.

Allow children to respond nonverbally by pointing to, picking up, showing, or giving something.

Read the whole book aloud in one language before reading it later in another language. Children are confused and lose interest when you alternate languages page by page.

Let children respond in their home languages, even when you ask a question in English or simply ask them to point to something.

Read books with repetitive patterns and phrases, encouraging children to complete the phrase when they are ready.

Children With Disabilities

You can adapt many of the strategies that you use for sharing stories and books with all children to build on the skills and interests of children with disabilities.

Strategies for Children With Partial Visual Impairments

Find well-lit, quiet, cozy places with few distractions.

Make sure the book faces the child directly.

Select picture books with large, simple pictures. Use big books and books with bright colors.

Engage children by having them hold and manipulate story objects. Let the child touch, feel, smell, listen to, and, if appropriate, taste the item. For example, if an apple is pictured in the book, offer a real apple for the child to explore.

Introduce "twin vision" books that have both printed and Braille text. These will help children with severely limited vision become aware that the bumps convey a message.

Help children explore "touch and feel" or "scratch and sniff" books. Many commercial "feely" books are available, but you can make some with large images.

Use recordings as another way for children to hear books being read. Find, make, or have families record favorite stories, and let children listen to them through headphones.

Share books that encourage children to move. For example, many movements accompany the words in Lorinda Bryan Cauley's book *Clap Your Hands.*

Responding to and Planning for Each Child

As you observe children interacting with stories and books, think about the objectives for development and learning. Consider what each child is learning and how you might respond. Here is how four teachers who are implementing *The Creative Curriculum*® use what they learn from their observations to respond to each child and to plan.

Observe	Reflect	Respond
Julio (4 months) and Linda are sitting together in the glider, reading a board book. A different animal is pictured on each page, and Linda tells him what each is called. As she turns each page, Julio squeals with delight and bangs his hands on the book. After a few minutes, he turns his head and pushes the book away.	Julio is showing interest in the speech of others (*Objective 8, Listens and understands increasingly complex language; Dimension a, Comprehends language*). He is using his body movements and vocalizations to communicate (*Objective 9, Uses language to express thoughts and needs; Dimension a, Uses an expanding expressive vocabulary*). He is actively manipulating books as they are read aloud (*Objective 17, Demonstrates knowledge of print and its uses; Dimension a, Uses and appreciates books*).	Linda notices Julio's nonverbal cues and says, "You are all done with the story." She closes the book and follows his gaze to see what caught his attention.
Willard (11 months) sits in Grace's lap as she reads him a counting book about babies. "One, two, three babies are smiling at me." As she reads each number, she bounces Willard gently on her knees. He laughs and turns the page.	Willard is continuing an activity when an adult interacts (*Objective 11, Demonstrates positive approaches to learning; Dimension a, Attends and engages*). He is engaging briefly with books as they are read aloud and finding pleasure in the experience (*Objective 17, Demonstrates knowledge of print and its uses; Dimension a, Uses and appreciates books*).	Grace acknowledges Willard's delight. "You like to bounce when we count the babies." She continues to read the book with Willard, bouncing him gently as she counts.

Observe	Reflect	Respond
"Let's look at the photo album your mother brought in today," Barbara suggests to Leo (18 months) as they settle down in a comfortable chair. She turns to the first picture and asks, "Where's Mommy?" Leo points to his mother, father, and himself in the picture, identifying, "Mommy. Daddy. Me, me."	Leo is using single words to communicate (*Objective 9, Uses language to express thoughts and needs*; *Dimension a, Uses an expanding expressive vocabulary*). He is recognizing and showing a beginning understanding of pictures (*Objective 17, Demonstrates knowledge of print and its uses*; *Dimension b, Uses print concepts*).	Barbara continues to ask Leo questions about the photos to encourage his language development. "What does your dog say?" Leo responds, "Woof, woof." Then Barbara asks "Who is this? Is she your grandma?"
Gena (30 months) is sitting in the book area with her doll, Molly. She picks up a favorite book and turns the pages, pointing at pictures and talking quietly to Molly. She continues even when Sam sits down beside her.	Gena is continuing an activity until her own goal is reached, despite distractions (*Objective 11, Demonstrates positive approaches to learning*; *Dimension a, Attends and engages*). She is pretending to read a favorite book (*Objective 18, Comprehends and responds to books*; *Dimension b, Uses emergent reading skills*).	Ivan observes Gena and writes a quick observation note. He also notices that Sam is interested in what she is doing. To encourage Gena to interact with other children, Ivan says, "Gena, I see that you are reading your book to Molly. Is it all right if Sam and I listen, too?"

Responsive Planning

In developing weekly plans, these teachers use their observations and refer to *Objectives for Development & Learning.* This is what they record on their weekly planning forms.

- On the "Child Planning Form," under "Current Information," Linda notes Julio's interest in the illustrations of animals. Under "Plans," she makes a note to bring in other books with animal pictures. On the "Group Planning Form," in the space for "Changes to the Environment," she lists the books that she will add to the bookshelf and book pockets.

- Grace records her observation about Willard on the "Child Planning Form," under "Current Information." She will focus on Willard's developing motor skills and interest in books by reading other stories that will encourage him to clap and turn the pages. On the "Group Planning Form," under "Changes to the Environment," Grace lists the books that she will add to the room. Under "Indoor Experiences," she notes that she will focus on adding motions as she reads to the children.

- Barbara thinks about how much Leo enjoyed looking at and talking about the photos of his family. On the "Group Planning Form," under "Family Involvement," she writes a reminder to ask families to bring photos from home. She will use the pictures to make individual books about each child's family to keep in the room.

- On the "Child Planning Form," Ivan records that Gena enjoyed reading to her doll and to other people. He makes a note under "Plans" to borrow a variety of books for the room from the public library. In the "Indoor Experiences" section on his "Group Planning Form," he writes a reminder to share the books each day during story times. Later he lists the books under "Changes to the Environment" so he will remember to add them to the bookshelf after he reads them to Gena and the other children.

Reading books and sharing your pleasure in language and stories are some of the most important experiences you can offer infants, toddlers, and twos. Children develop a foundation for literacy when they regularly hear books read aloud and have opportunities to explore them firsthand. Their love for books will continually enrich their experiences and stretch their imaginations and dreams. The letter to families is a way to offer ideas about sharing stories and books with their children.

Dear Families:

Everyone agrees that books are a necessary part of a child's education. Even young infants benefit from having simple books read to them! Looking at books and hearing them read aloud stimulate an infant's brain development in important ways.

Before children learn to read, they need to know a lot about language, how a story progresses, and how books work. Children who learn to love books are more likely to become successful learners and lifelong readers. In our program, we offer your child a wide variety of good books, and we read together every day.

What You Can Do at Home

Read and tell stories to your child every day. The words and pictures are important, but, most of all, spending time with you as you read aloud and tell stories lets your child know how much you value these activities. Reading is a wonderful way to be together, whether during your child's bedtime routine or a relaxed daytime opportunity.

Here are some suggestions for reading with your child.

- **Pick a story that you enjoy.** Share rhymes, songs, and stories from your childhood. Your enthusiasm will be contagious. Start by talking about the book's cover or simply by beginning to read.

- **Talk about the pictures.** You do not always have to read a story from beginning to end.

- **Ask your child questions as you read.** Have your child find an object in a picture, for example, "Where is the dog's ball?" Take cues from your child's gestures, sounds, or words, for example, "Yes, that's the baby's Grandma, just like Nona Maria." As your child is able to follow a story, you can ask more open-ended questions. For example, you might ask, "What do you think will happen next?" or "What did you like best about the story?"

- **Be prepared to vary the length of your reading sessions.** Your child might want you to read a story again and again, but you also need to be prepared to stop at any point. There is no need to force your child to be still while you read. Sometimes children want to be more active. Stop when your child no longer seems interested.

Let us share. We can give you the titles of the books your child enjoys here, and you can tell us your child's current favorite books and rhymes at home. We would also love to have you record your child's favorite story or nursery rhyme so we can play it for your child here. We will be glad to help you make the recording. Together, we can help prepare your child to be a lifelong reader.

Sincerely,

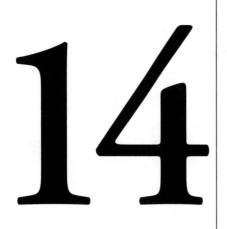

14

Connecting With Music and Movement

Supporting Development and Learning 308

Creating an Environment for Music and Movement 309
Selecting and Displaying Materials 309

Caring and Teaching 311
Responding to and Planning for Each Child 314

Sharing Thoughts About Music and Movement 317

Connecting With Music and Movement

Jasmine (8 months) is sitting on the floor, bouncing to some music. Janet says, "It looks as though you want to dance." She sits next to Jasmine and joins her in moving to the beat. They smile at one another. Then Janet holds out her arms and asks, "Would you like to dance?" When Jasmine reaches toward her, Janet picks her up and begins dancing across the room. Jasmine laughs and bounces up and down in Janet's arms.

Most people enjoy listening to, creating, and moving to music. Music affects our emotions and inspires movement. Newborn infants can often be comforted by the rhythmic sound of an adult's heart as they are held closely, or by being rocked steadily or bounced gently. By the time they can sit, infants often bob their heads and torsos or move their arms to music.

Just as toddlers and twos want to hear favorite stories again and again, they like to hear and sing favorite songs repeatedly. You may hear toddlers and twos chorus refrains such as "E-I-E-I-O" as they play. They love to make music by hitting a pot with a spoon or by playing real instruments, and they enjoy moving to different tempos and rhythms.

As infants, toddlers, and twos move to music in different ways, they stretch their bodies and imaginations. Whether they move their hands in fingerplays or move their whole bodies as they dance, children respond to the rhythm and beat of music and the related words. You can offer spontaneous and planned music and movement experiences that encourage listening, singing, fingerplay, dancing, and other ways of moving and making music.

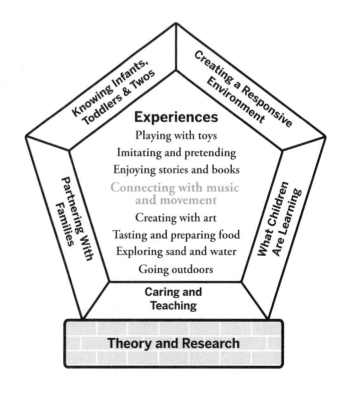

Supporting Development and Learning

Children develop social–emotional, physical, cognitive, and language skills as they engage with music and movement.

Learning about themselves and others: As you dance with an infant in your arms; take her to the changing table, singing, "This is the way we change your diaper"; or hum a lullaby to help her fall asleep, you are building a relationship that fosters trust. Familiar songs and songs with children's names can be part of hello and good-bye rituals. They help children feel safe and often help them feel connected to their absent families. Simple songs, such as "If You're Happy and You Know It," can help toddlers and twos label their feelings. As children sing together or parade in a group, banging on drums and shaking maracas, they learn to share music with others.

Learning about moving: When infants, toddlers, and twos hear music, they often respond by moving their bodies. They may kick excitedly, bounce on your knee as you cuddle and sing, or march around the room to a favorite recording. Young children learn to move through space and practice basic gross-motor skills as they respond to various kinds of music. Over time, they learn to move their legs, feet, arms, hands, heads, hips, and torsos quickly and slowly, up and down, in and out, and over and under. They also sharpen their fine-motor skills as their hands open and shut in simple fingerplays.

Learning about the world: Young children learn about position in space and build memory and sequencing skills as they participate in musical experiences that encourage them to move, change positions, and perform movements in a particular order. When infants shake a rattle or press a button to hear a sound, they are learning about cause and effect. Children also gain important background knowledge through songs. They sing about wheels going 'round and 'round and Old McDonald's farm animals.

Learning about communicating: Music and movement experiences also play an important role in language and literacy development. Infants' early coos and babbles have musical qualities, as do the conversational duets they share with you. Songs can be used to promote an awareness of sounds and to encourage children to experiment with language. You call attention to the features of sounds, such as pitch (high-low), volume (loud-soft), and tempo (fast-slow). Songs, rhymes, and fingerplays are wonderful ways to help children extend language and build vocabulary, such as when you explain the itsy-bitsy spider's waterspout, help children learn that stars twinkle, and anticipate the moment when the players all fall down!

Creating an Environment for Music and Movement

Organize a safe open space for dancing and moving. It must be large enough so that children will not bump into anything or each other. This space may be used for other activities as well.

Choose a carpeted area if possible, because young children like to fall down intentionally. Carpeting also helps to absorb sounds, as do cushions.

Include comfortable adult seating, such as a glider, so you can rock babies to music.

Place a radio, tape recorder, or compact disc player (and cords) close to an electrical outlet and out of children's reach.

Use the outdoor environment as another setting for music and movement experiences. Simple games that involve identifying outdoor sounds help children develop listening skills. There is enough space outdoors for children to move freely and to join simple circle games.

Selecting and Displaying Materials

In addition to your voice and enthusiasm, you need a variety of musical selections, equipment for playing recordings, and materials for children to make their own instruments. Young children tend to prefer music and songs that have a strong rhythm, repetition, and nonsense words; evoke a mood (such as calm or lively); suggest different movements; and tell a story. There are many wonderful recordings of music for children, ranging from traditional favorites to new songs.

Expand your musical choices beyond those selections recorded specifically for children. If possible, introduce a variety of styles: classical, country, folk, reggae, rock and roll, and jazz. Include music from a variety of cultures, as well as other styles you enjoy, so the children hear different melodies and rhythms. Supplement your collection with materials from the library and from families. Many public libraries have selections of tapes and compact discs. Families may also be able to provide music that shares their individual preferences and cultures.

Young Infants

Include toys for young infants that make musical sounds. Hang musical mobiles, and give babies wrist and ankle bells to hold. Babies' random movements soon become intentional as they learn that they can make sounds by moving things. Offer toys that make sounds as children use them, such as balls with bells inside or push-and-pull toys that make musical sounds as they roll along.

Mobile Infants, Toddlers, and Twos

Young children use their bodies as their first rhythm instruments, but you will want to offer other simple rhythm instruments. Possibilities include drums, xylophones, large bells, clackers, rattles and shakers, tambourines, maracas, cymbals, and wood blocks. These allow children to create and respond to music as they bang, ring, swish, and click. Make sure that anything with small objects inside or attached, such as a shaker or a bell, does not present a choking hazard.

You can also make your own instruments. For example, make drums from oatmeal boxes and cymbals from metal pie pans. Make rattles and shakers by filling containers with rice, macaroni, or buttons and fastening them very securely. You can also turn pots and pans upside down, offer wooden spoons, and observe as children experiment with different rhythms and sounds.

Store the instruments in clear plastic containers so children can see them. For variety, rotate the instruments that are available to the children. As with all materials, offer several of each type to minimize problems with sharing. Providing duplicates is more important than having a wide variety.

Add picture book versions of children's favorite songs and fingerplays to your book collection. Some sets include cassettes or CDs. Include books that call attention to indoor and outdoor sounds, tell stories about the joy of singing and dancing, encourage children to clap their hands, or make suggestions about ways to move.

Caring and Teaching

Sharing your own appreciation of music and movement will inspire children to participate joyfully. You do not need to be a great singer to delight young children with music. Focus on the fun of singing together. Sing short, simple, familiar songs. Remember that young children are likely to ask for their favorite songs repeatedly. Make up new songs about the children and about familiar things, people, and events. Children love to hear songs with their names and to laugh at the silly songs you make up about what they are doing. Listen and respond when you hear children singing their own versions of familiar tunes.

Music can be a part of many routines and experiences. Play soft music for children at nap time and sing to them during routines such as dressing, diapering, and toileting. Promote children's attention and listening skills by playing music selectively and inviting a child or two to listen with you for a few minutes. If you play music constantly, it becomes background noise that children tend to ignore after a while. Play music for short periods throughout the day, to remind children that it is time to clean up, to encourage a child's gross-motor movement, and to soothe an upset child.

Help children learn concepts through simple games, songs, and fingerplays. As children circle and fall during "Ring a Round the Rosie," or feel their toes when you play "This Little Piggy," they are learning new language, concepts, social skills, and physical skills.

Music is a wonderful way to help children feel connected to their families during the time they spend with you. Ask families about the songs they sing at home and the kinds of music that they like. Learn the lullabies that a family croons at bedtime. Include music from the children's home cultures and in different languages, as possible. Share equipment with family members so they can record songs for you to play while their children are in your care.

Young Infants

Young infants respond to music and other sounds by turning their heads, smiling, laughing, and moving their arms and legs. They are usually calmed by soft, rhythmic sounds, such as lullabies, and by the voices of familiar teachers. They tend to respond in more energetic ways when music is lively. Keep in mind that some infants are more sensitive than others to sounds and may be overstimulated by music that other infants enjoy.

> **Julio** (4 months) is fussy. Linda picks him up and sings softly to him as she sits with him in the glider. He quiets and gazes at her. She smiles and asks, "Are you feeling better, now? Do you want to sing some more?" As Linda continues rocking and singing, she gives Julio a positive experience with music and movement.

- Sing short, simple songs to infants in a high, quiet voice: *Mama's little baby loves shortening, shortening. Mama's little baby loves shortening bread.*

- Comment upon the child's response: *You like it when we dance together. Here we go, back and forth, back and forth.*

- Call the child's attention to interesting sounds: *Those wind chimes are making music for us. Listen.*

- Repeat sounds an infant makes: *Da, da, da. You're singing your da-da song.*

Mobile Infants

To promote children's increasing skills, conduct music and movement experiences with one or two children at a time. These experiences include playing rhythm instruments, dancing, and singing during daily routines and play experiences. Sing while changing a child's diaper or dressing to go outdoors.

> **Willard** (11 months) and **Abby** (14 months) enjoy the sounds and music that are part of their daily lives. For example, Willard waits for Grace to walk her fingers up his belly while she sings, "The Itsy-Bitsy Spider." Abby beams with pleasure when Brooks sings, 'Where is Abby? Where is Abby?' to the tune of the fingerplay "Where is Thumbkin?"

As their language skills improve, some mobile infants will join you as you sing. Sometimes they repeat sounds over and over, such as "B-B-B-B" or "da-da, da-da, da-da." They may half-babble and half-talk as they sing a familiar song such as "Baa, Baa, Black Sheep." With their increasing balance and physical coordination, they also enjoy playing simple rhythm instruments and moving to the beat.

As you interact with mobile infants, you can promote both their pleasure in and learning from music and movement. Here are some ways to help children focus on their experiences:

- Encourage children to respond to music physically: *You are moving slowly to this slow music.*

- Call a child's attention to common sounds: *Do you hear the clock ticking?*

- Identify different sounds: *The drum is beating in this marching music. It goes, "Boom, boom, boom."*

- Teach simple fingerplays, such as "Open, Shut Them" and "The Wheels on the Bus."

- Vary the speed at which you chant rhymes. Sing *"Pat-a-Cake"* very slowly and then more quickly, giving the child an opportunity to tap your outstretched hands to the beat.

- Move with the child to the beat: As you gently bounce the child on your knee, sing, *One baby monkey jumping on the bed.*

Toddlers

With your encouragement, toddlers will pay attention to the sounds around them, and you might see them running to the window to listen to a chirping bird or a passing plane. They have learned to discriminate among many sounds, and they can match the sound *moo* to a picture of a cow and the sound *meow* to a picture of a cat. They are also fascinated by the nonverbal sounds that they can produce. Practically anything can become a musical instrument, so toddlers experiment with shaking, tapping, banging, hitting, and pounding a variety of objects.

Toddlers continue to sing and to enjoy music and fingerplays as social experiences. They have discovered songs that they particularly like and want to repeat them again and again. They hum and sing as they play, and they make up simple two-pitch songs.

As their fine and gross-motor skills develop, toddlers have more control over their bodies. This allows them to experiment with various kinds of movement.

Here are some ways to interact with toddlers during music and movement experiences and other opportunities to listen:

- Encourage a child's enjoyment of songs: *Shall we play the animal song you like so much?*

- Nurture their interest in environmental sounds: *You hear the rain blowing against the window.*

- Encourage toddlers to sing familiar songs: *Is today your baby's birthday? Are you going to sing "Happy Birthday" to him?*

- Focus children's attention on the way they move: *Can you move quickly to the beat of this drum?*

- Help them discriminate among different sounds: *Listen carefully. Do you hear the bird on the windowsill? Now do you hear a barking dog?*

- Use music and movement experiences to build a positive relationship: *Let's hold hands and stomp through the leaves together.*

Twos

Two-year-olds love rhythm and repetition. They have become good listeners, responsive to music with complex patterns. They move their whole bodies in different ways to various kinds of music, jumping, bouncing, falling, and swaying. They love to twirl and fall like autumn leaves, spinning tops, or tired children. Dance with the children, sometimes holding hands or letting them stand on your feet as you move to the music. Help children focus on rhythm by clapping, stomping, or shaking a tambourine to the beat of songs and rhymes.

Twos begin to sing some of the lyrics of familiar songs. They can fill in words when you pause, just as they complete a sentence in a story, especially when the song includes rhyme and repetition. You may also hear them singing catchy jingles they hear on TV and the radio. Encourage twos to create original songs. Sing along when you hear them singing a made-up song while putting their dolls to sleep. Encourage them to create new verses for their favorite songs. "Daddy's taking me to the zoo tomorrow" can soon be "Daddy's taking me to school tomorrow" or "Momma's taking me to the store today."

Two-year-olds often enjoy singing or listening to music during a brief small-group time. Remember to keep group times short, and expect and allow children to come and go as they wish. Here are some ideas for encouraging 2-year-olds to have fun with music and movement.

- Stimulate their imaginations: *Let's pretend we are pancakes. Let's flip in the pan.*

- Use songs as part of daily routines: *Let's sing your good-bye song to Daddy.*

- Introduce more complicated fingerplays, using hands and two fingers: *Two little ducks went out to play, over the river and far away.*

- Omit a word and let the children fill in the blank: *If you're happy and you know it, clap your_____.*

- Encourage a child to explore ways to make music: *That tambourine made a loud sound when you hit it with your hand. Does it make another kind of sound?*

Responding to and Planning for Each Child

As you observe young children during music and movement experiences, think about the objectives for development and learning. Consider what each child is learning and how you might respond. Here is how four teachers who are implementing *The Creative Curriculum®* use what they learn from their observations to respond to each child and to plan.

Observe	Reflect	Respond
Linda holds Julio (4 months) as she rocks him in the glider. She sings, "Duérmete mi niño. Duérmete mi sol. Duérmete pedazo, De mi corazón. Go to sleep my baby. Go to sleep my sunshine. You will always be in this heart of mine." Julio gazes at Linda as she sings. His body relaxes, and his eyes begin to close.	Julio is beginning to develop his own pattern for sleeping (*Objective 1, Regulates own emotions and behaviors*; *Dimension c, Takes care of own needs appropriately*) He is showing an interest in the speech of others (*Objective 8, Listens and understands increasingly complex language*; *Dimension a, Comprehends language*).	Linda continues to sing and rock Julio until she sees that he is ready to go to sleep. She gently lays him in his crib as she continues to sing softly. Julio drifts off to sleep as Linda notes the time on his family's communication log.
Willard (11 months) watches as Grace puts a CD in the CD player. He smiles when the music starts, bounces up and down, and babbles, "Du-du-du."	Willard is discovering that repeated actions yield similar effects (*Objective 12, Remembers and connects experiences*; *Dimension b, Makes connections*). He is babbling and combining sounds to communicate (*Objective 9, Uses language to express thoughts and needs*; *Dimension a, Uses an expanding expressive vocabulary*)	Grace acknowledges Willard's interest, "Willard, I see you smiling and dancing. You must like the music." To encourage his language development, she imitates his sounds, "Du-du-du. You are singing with the music. Du-du-du."

Observe	Reflect	Respond
Leo (18 months) sits on the floor with a xylophone. He hits the colored keys with the mallet, one by one. He looks at Barbara and laughs.	Leo is learning how objects can be used by handling them (*Objective 11, Demonstrates positive approaches to learning; Dimension e, Shows flexibility and inventiveness in thinking*). He explores ways to make something happen (*Objective 11, Demonstrates positive approaches to learning; Dimension d, Shows curiosity and motivation*).	Barbara encourages Leo's interest in the xylophone by saying, "Leo, I hear you making music." As he hits another key, Barbara raises the pitch of her voice and says, "You made a high note." He hits another key and looks at her. "You made a low note," she says, lowering her pitch.
Jonisha (33 months) sits under a tree on the playground, watching leaves blow in the wind. Later, inside the room, LaToya turns on some music. Jonisha waves her arms around, rocks her body back and forth, and spins in a circle. She says, "Look! I'm a leaf!"	Jonisha is using simple sentences with three or more words (*Objective 9, Uses language to express thoughts and needs; Dimension c, Uses conventional grammar*). She is making use of imaginary objects in pretend play (*Objective 14, Uses symbols and images to represent something not present; Dimension b, Engages in sociodramatic play*).	LaToya acknowledges Jonisha's play by saying, "You are moving like those leaves on the windy playground." To support Jonisha's language development, LaToya says, "Those leaves were swirling around and around in the wind. They were and moving just the way you are moving now."

Responsive Planning

In developing weekly plans, these teachers use their observations and refer to *Objectives for Development & Learning.* This is what they record on their weekly planning forms.

- On the "Child Planning Form," Linda notes Julio's response to the lullaby she sang in Spanish. Under "Plans," she writes that she will ask Julio's mother and grandmother to teach her another Spanish song that she can sing to Julio.

- On the "Child Planning Form," Grace writes a note about Willard's dancing and singing to the music. Under "Plans," she writes that she will play various types of music to find out what he likes and that she will talk to him about the sounds and rhythms he is hearing. On the "Group Planning Form," under "Family Involvement," she writes a reminder to encourage families to bring recordings of their favorite music so that she can share them with the children.

- As Barbara reviews her observation notes for the week, she sees that several children enjoyed using the two new xylophones she added to the display last week. On the "Group Planning Form," under "Changes to the Environment," she notes that she will add a few small drums and some maracas. Under "Outdoor Experiences," she writes that she will bring the instruments outside for the children to use on Monday and Tuesday.

- On the "Child Planning Form," under "Current Information," LaToya writes about Jonisha's creative movement experience. Under "Plans," she writes that she will bring in some long streamers and scarves that Jonisha might enjoy waving while she dances.

Music and movement are joyful experiences for children. As you rock babies to a gentle lullaby, sing a favorite song from your own childhood, or dance around the room with a toddler, you share special moments with children. The letter to families is a way to offer ideas about sharing music and movement with their children.

Dear Families:

Listening and moving to music are important for children. Newborns are comforted when they are rocked or gently bounced to a steady rhythm. Older infants, toddlers, and twos have favorite songs and love making music by banging a pot with a spoon. In addition to being pleasurable, these experiences are important to children's overall development. Here are some examples of what children learn.

When your child ...	Your child is learning...
• is soothed when you play soft music	• to comfort himself
• holds hands and dances with another child	• about playing with other children
• stomps around the room to a march	• to use his large muscles
• joins a fingerplay	• fine-motor skills

What You Can Do at Home

It's easy to make music and movement a part of your child's life. Here are some suggestions to try at home.

• **Call your child's attention to a variety of sounds.** Listen to the ticking clock and a singing bird, and talk about them.

• **Sing to your child.** Start with simple songs, including those that you particularly enjoy.

• **Make up songs with your child.** To start, use a familiar tune and just substitute a few words, such as a person's name or an event. For example, you might sing, "Sarah had a little doll, little doll, little doll…"

• **Play different types of music.** In addition to children's music, your child may enjoy listening to a variety of melodies and rhythms: folk songs, reggae, jazz, classical music, popular music, and so on.

• **Move and dance together.** It's fun to take giant steps and then tiny steps during a walk. You can even try to hop like a frog or wiggle like a worm!

• **Offer your child simple rhythm instruments.** You can make a drum from an oatmeal box, cymbals from metal pie pans, and shakers by filling containers with rice or buttons and fastening them securely. Your kitchen is a child's orchestra. Listen as your child bangs on your pots, pans, and unbreakable bowls.

It doesn't matter whether you can carry a tune or play an instrument. Sharing your enjoyment of music and movement with your child does matter. We'll be happy to share the songs we sing, and we'd love to learn some of your family's favorites.

Sincerely,

Creating With Art

Supporting Development and Learning 320

Creating an Environment for Art 321
Selecting Materials for Different Ages 321
Setting Up and Displaying Materials 326

Caring and Teaching 328
Inappropriate Art Activities 331
Responding to and Planning for Each Child 332

**Sharing Thoughts About
Art Experiences** 335

Creating With Art

Brooks helps Abby (14 months) put on a smock and says, "Abby, I see you are ready to help me make some squishy Cloud Dough today." Abby nods, and Brooks places a bowl of flour along with plastic pitchers of pre-measured salad oil and water on the table. Abby, who is familiar with the process, looks up at Brooks expectantly. As Brooks begins to pour the flour into the mixing bowl, Abby extends her arm into the stream of flour and squeals with delight. Brooks encourages, "Doesn't the flour feel cool and soft? It's going to feel very different when we finish making the dough."

Art for infants, toddlers, and twos is largely a sensory experience. A young infant strokes the fringe on a stuffed animal and relaxes contentedly. A mobile infant joyfully tears colored tissue paper and waves the pieces in the air. A toddler squeals with delight as she moves her fingers through smooth finger paint. Twos are beginning to understand that pictures, models, and constructions represent people and things. A 2-year-old pokes, pounds, and then rolls out a lump of playdough and proudly shows you how he mixed two colors together to make marbled dough. Young children are interested in what different materials are like and what they can do with them. They are not intent on making a product (as older children can be). Painting lines on paper with a brush and tearing paper into pieces are satisfying experiences by themselves.

When you provide a variety of art experiences for young children, they discover that certain materials feel interesting and are fun to use. They also learn that they can control and make marks with a variety of tools and materials. Older twos are beginning to understand that the pictures, models, and constructions they make can represent people and things. The everyday art experiences you offer infants, toddlers, and twos build a foundation for both appreciating and creating through art.

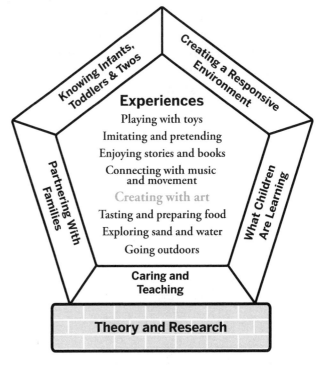

Supporting Development and Learning

Art experiences are a wonderful way for infants, toddlers, and twos to develop their social–emotional, physical, cognitive, and language skills.

Learning about themselves and others: Art materials give children a safe, constructive way to express their feelings, as when they pound dough with their fists or swirl their fingers through paint. Older twos feel a sense of accomplishment when they triumphantly make their first snips with scissors or tell you that their drawing is a picture of a cat.

Learning about moving: When you provide a wide variety of tools and materials for art experiences, young children build their fine-motor skills. Holding a crayon and making a mark is a sign that mobile infants are learning to control their small muscles. When toddlers paste a feather on a collage, they are demonstrating eye-hand coordination. As children's small muscles and eye-hand coordination develop, they are able to use smaller and more refined tools for art experiences.

Learning about the world: The world is full of surprises for infants, toddlers, and twos, and experimenting with art materials is another way to learn about objects. Put a sheet of clear adhesive paper on the wall and let children find out that some objects stick. Let a toddler dip a comb in paint and notice that it makes a print on paper. Give twos a large paint brush, a bucket of water, and an outside wall to paint, and watch their surprise as the wall darkens. All of these discoveries help children learn about objects and about cause and effect. When a 2-year-old scribbles on a page and decides afterward that he made a picture of a puppy, he is beginning to understand that he can use art materials to represent something.

Learning about communicating: As you talk with children about what they are doing, seeing, and feeling during an art experience, you help build their understanding of language and give them interesting new words. You might say, "That *goop* is *sticky*," "fingerpaint is *smooth*," and "playdough is *squishy*." The vocabulary of textures is vast: *rough, smooth, bumpy, itchy, velvety,* and so on. Art is related to stories and books as well. Many books for very young children focus on naming colors, animals, people, and common objects. As you read a variety of books with children, talk about the illustrations so that they begin to understand that pictures are meaningful.

Creating an Environment for Art

The materials you select should correspond to children's interests and abilities. Beginning art experiences are a part of everyday explorations for young infants, so they do not need a special place for art. Mobile infants and young toddlers need some bare floor space or a child-sized table on which to draw, paint, print, mold, tear, and paste. Older toddlers and twos are ready for a protected space where they can choose and use art materials.

Selecting Materials for Different Ages

The best art materials for infants, toddlers, and twos are those that invite exploration and experimentation.

Young Infants

With common materials, you can give young infants the kinds of experiences that nurture an interest in exploring and experimenting. All the sensory experiences you offer are a foundation for later art experiences. Place some fabric scraps within their reach, such as swatches of flannel, corduroy, satin, silk, taffeta, netting, knits, hosiery, denim, fleece, lace, fake fur, and burlap. Once infants are able to sit, they enjoy playing with various types of nontoxic papers that they can crumple, tear, shred, and wave in the air. Pieces of waxed paper, butcher paper, parchment, rice paper, and tissue paper provide different experiences.

Mobile Infants

These additional materials will be of interest to mobile infants.

Finger painting—Have a slick table surface on which infants may paint directly with their hands, or you can cover the table with oilcloth or vinyl. They can also paint directly on cafeteria trays.

Painting with water—Children can use stubby-handled brushes (5–6 inches long) to paint with water on fences and the outside walls of buildings.

Drawing—Give mobile infants jumbo crayons and chalk. Provide large sheets of sturdy paper. Outdoors, children can use chalk on blackboards, sidewalks, and blacktops.

Molding—Substances like Cloud Dough or Basic Playdough work best because they can be squeezed easily.

Cloud Dough

6 cups flour

1 cup salad oil

water to bind (approximately 1 cup)

Knead ingredients together. Final product will feel oily and very smooth. Store in an airtight container.

Basic Playdough

3 cups flour

1 cup salt

1 cup water

1/4 cup salad oil

Knead all ingredients together. Form into balls. Store in an airtight container.

Baker's Clay

4 cups flour

1 cup salt

1 1/2 cups warm water

Mix all ingredients together. Shape into a ball. Store in an airtight container.

Toddlers

The same materials used by mobile infants will interest toddlers, who also enjoy some additional materials.

Painting—Provide flat bristled brushes (5–6 inches long) with nylon hair and stubby handles. Large paper (about 24 inches x 36 inches or larger) allows toddlers to paint with broad, pumping motions. Include newsprint, manila, and butcher paper of various sizes and shapes. Try covering an entire table with butcher paper to give children a broad canvas. Toddlers like to paint at a table or a tilted surface that is low to the ground, such as a low easel. When you first introduce paint to toddlers, limit the choice to two colors. A greater variety of colors can be offered later.

Tempera Paint for One Child

2 1/2 ounces water

1–2 teaspoons Tempera paint (any color)

3 drops liquid dish detergent such as Ivory®

Pour all ingredients into an empty juice can. Stir with tongue depressor.

Finger painting—Use cafeteria trays, mirrored surfaces with protected edges, or plastic wrap taped to table and floor surfaces. Children can also finger paint directly on a table as younger children do. In addition to commercial finger paint, consider making your own with liquid starch. Nontoxic shaving cream is another interesting material for children to explore with their fingers.

You can also try making Goop.

Goop

3 cups corn starch

2 cups warm water

Gradually add water to corn starch. Mix ingredients together with hands. Goop is ready to use when it changes from being lumpy to satiny.

Goop hardens in the air and turns to liquid when held. It resists punching, but a light touch causes a finger to sink in.

Drawing—Toddlers can use all the materials already listed for mobile infants, plus water-based felt-tip markers. Provide both white and colored papers.

Molding—Toddlers enjoy dough of different textures and colors. They can use an eyedropper filled with liquid food coloring to add color to the dough and then work the color in with their fingers and fists. Provide a few utensils to extend the molding experience for children, such as a potato masher or blocks of different shapes.

Twos

While 2-year-olds enjoy the same materials as younger children, they use them with greater skill and in new ways. Encourage their explorations by adding a few additional tools and materials.

Molding—Offer children basic tools, such as wooden mallets, tongue depressors, plastic rods cut to 6-inch lengths, a wooden dowel for rolling out dough, and a garlic press. You can also involve twos in helping to prepare the dough. Once cooked playdough hardens, children can paint what they created.

Cooked Playdough

2 cups corn starch

1 cup baking soda

1 cup water

Mix all ingredients together and cook over medium heat. Stir constantly until mixture forms a ball. Allow to cool slightly and knead. Store in plastic wrap in the refrigerator.

Drawing and painting—Give twos different types of papers. Each type provides a different experience. You might offer several of these:

- poster paper of various colors, sizes, and shapes
- tissue paper of various colors, sizes, and shapes
- crepe paper of various colors, sizes, and shapes
- corrugated cardboard of various colors, sizes, and shapes
- finger painting paper coated with buttermilk, liquid starch, or sugar water (great for chalk)
- butcher paper

You can also offer a variety of objects and tools, in addition to paint brushes:

- feathers
- twigs or leaves
- eyedroppers
- foam rubber brushes
- toothbrushes
- vegetable and pastry brushes
- sponges

Vary the texture and smell of paint for a variety of painting experiences. As you prepare tempera and finger paint, try changing its quality by adding one or more of the following items.

Adding this...	Makes paint...
flour	lumpy
Karo™ syrup	shiny and sticky
sand or sawdust	rough and gritty
Epsom salt	sparkly
liquid soap	slimy

Printing—This may be a new activity for twos. Make pads by fastening a piece of firm foam rubber or a sponge onto a Styrofoam™ meat tray. Then pour tempera paint onto the foam or sponge. Collect tissue paper, butcher paper, newsprint, and a variety of colored and textured papers for children to use for printing. Provide objects such as rubber stamps, sponges, and corks leaves to dip into the pad and press onto the paper.

Collage Making—Collect colorful yarn; ribbons; papers with assorted textures and colors; magazines and catalogs; scraps of material; leaves, dried flowers, and weeds; and recycled gift wrapping, greeting cards, and post cards. To assemble the collage, use library paste and, if appropriate, give children small, blunt-nosed scissors (4 inches and 4 1/2 inches long).

Setting Up and Displaying Materials

Organize the environment to minimize messes while encouraging children's exploration and creativity. Here are some suggestions for setting up.

Locate the area near a sink. If no sink is available nearby, you can bring buckets of water to your art area for preliminary cleaning up. Fill empty hand lotion or liquid soap dispensers with water for initial handwashing and later help children wash their hands thoroughly at the sink. Eventually, twos can help wash paint brushes and wipe off the table surface where they have been finger painting.

Protect the floor and other surfaces. Use an old shower curtain or a painter's drop cloth to protect the floor from spills and drips. Cleaning equipment such as mops, paper towels, a broom, and a dust pan should be within close reach. Squeegees like those used to wash windows are also helpful for removing finger paint from tables.

Protect children's clothing. Children should wear smocks to protect their clothing from messy materials. You can purchase smocks or make them from old shirts or oilcloth.

Provide surfaces at different heights. Mobile infants and toddlers can explore materials on the floor, as well as while sitting or standing at a low table. Toddlers and twos also enjoy painting at a large low easel.

Keep some materials out of reach. Certain types of materials should be stored on high shelves or in storage cabinets where children cannot reach them. These include materials that you need to prepare (paints and collage items) or that require close supervision (paste and scissors).

Display art materials for toddlers and twos on a low shelf. Materials like playdough, paper, crayons, and chalk can be displayed in containers on a low shelf where children can choose what they want. Label containers and shelves with pictures and words so children can find and return materials.

Storage Ideas

- Use empty frozen juice containers as paint containers. Cover them with different colors of bright adhesive paper and fill them halfway with the corresponding color of paint. Make a paint caddy by placing the containers in a cardboard six-pack container with a handle.

- Keep modeling dough and clay in covered plastic containers.

- Use baskets or plastic containers to hold chalk and crayons.

- Keep felt-tip markers upside down in their caps. For more permanent storage, pour plaster of Paris into a jelly-roll pan or tray. When the plaster starts to set, place the marker caps upside down in it. After the plaster has hardened, return the markers to their caps.

- Turn egg cartons upside down and poke holes for storing blunt-nose scissors or short-handled paintbrushes.

- Use an empty coffee can to hold scissors or brushes. Punch holes in the plastic lid of the can and cover the edges of the holes with masking tape so children cannot cut their fingers.

Display children's artwork. Even though toddlers and twos are more interested in exploring what they can do with art materials than in finishing a painting or drawing, save some of their work for portfolios and to display in the room. Post selected works where the children will see them, for instance, on the bottom of a wall or room divider. To protect their work, you can buy clear Plexiglas® frames or sheets.

Caring and Teaching

While there are some differences in the kinds of art experiences you offer infants and those you plan for toddlers and twos, the process of using art materials is more important than what children produce with them. The goal is to make it possible for children to explore and experiment freely with a variety of materials.

To plan art experiences, review what you know about the children in your group. What do they most enjoy? What new skills are they developing? Who enjoys messy activities? Who avoids them? Keep in mind that the younger the child, the more gross-motor skills are involved in art experiences. When mobile infants paint the play yard fence with water, they use their whole bodies to make broad strokes. Twos have developed more wrist and hand control, so they use their arms, hands, and fingers to paint, rather than their whole bodies.

Young Infants

You probably already have many materials in your indoor and outdoor environments that infants can touch, smell, look at, and even chew on. Allow time for infants to explore what interests them.

> **Julio** (4 months), while sitting on Linda's lap, becomes fascinated by the texture of her scarf. Noticing this interest, Linda allows him to play with it as long as he likes.

See what happens when an infant discovers a dab of yogurt on her tray. Observe how she uses her fingers, hands, and wrists to explore its smooth texture. As young infants explore the world through their senses, talk about what they are experiencing.

- The sensory experience: *That yogurt feels smooth.*
- The child's actions: *You're making lines in the yogurt.*
- The child's feelings: *You certainly are having a good time with that yogurt!*

Share joyful moments of discovery together and focus on what the child is doing. You will gain insight into the infant's developing skills and interests, and this information helps you plan future experiences for the child.

Mobile Infants

Mobile infants can grasp a crayon or brush, and paint with water on a chalkboard, wall, or fence. Begin by offering fat, stubby crayons that mobile infants can grasp with their whole hand. Do not expect an infant to hold the crayon with thumb and fingers or to be able to draw using wrist movements. At this stage of development, drawing usually involves a lot of arm movement and sometimes whole body movement.

Offer the child a crayon or let her select one. She will probably be as interested in the way it feels and smells as she is interested in its color and what she can do with it. Tape a large piece of paper (at least 24 x 36 inches) to the floor. Then gently show the child how to use the crayon by guiding his hand.

Introduce older mobile infants to painting with water in much the same way, because children go through the same developmental steps in painting as they do in drawing. They paint with bold arm movements, using their entire arms and bodies.

For molding experiences, children need the freedom to poke, pound, and squeeze the dough. Handling molding materials is both soothing and filled with learning opportunities about the use of objects and about cause and effect.

When you make dough with children, notice what intrigues them and build on their interests.

- Comment on their actions: *You sure can squeeze that Cloud Dough hard.*
- Help them solve a problem: *It's getting sticky. Should we add some more flour?*
- Talk about their reaction: *You like it better when the dough isn't so sticky.*
- Engage the child's cooperation: *What a big helper you are in cleaning up!*

Toddlers

Many of the same art experiences you offer mobile infants are appropriate for toddlers. Because they have more control over their small muscles, they can begin to paint and draw with a variety of tools. Toddlers are more aware of what they are doing and understand you when you talk with them about their experiences.

Organize experiences so that toddlers can experiment and use materials without having too many constraints. Then interact in ways that show you are interested in what they are doing and make suggestions to extend their ideas.

- Describe what the child is doing: *You painted lots of lines on the ground with your water and paintbrush.*

- Make suggestions to extend the experience: *Do you want to paint anything else? I see a fence and a table. They might need some painting.*

- Provide choices: *What color should we make our dough today? We have red, yellow, and blue food coloring.*

- Reflect a child's feelings: *I thought you would enjoy the feel of that Goop we made! It's kind of sticky, isn't it?*

Twos

Twos happily use the same materials in different ways, but they also begin to take an interest in what they are producing. Because they have developed greater wrist control, they can control their scribbling. Their lines become curves, spirals, ovals, and eventually circles. They may start making designs, repeating them, and sometimes seeing patterns in what they made. While the patterns may be totally unplanned, they are exciting for a child to discover. These experiences also affect children's thinking. For example, they learn about predicting ("If I use paste, the object will stick"); about space ("If I squeeze this much paint out of the bottle, the paint runs off the paper"); about transformation ("If I add yellow paint to red paint, it looks different"); and about cause and effect ("If I rub the paint brush against the edge of the bottle, paint will not drip down the brush").

Some twos have enough muscle control to use paste and scissors.

Jonisha (33 months) proudly tears magazine pages into tiny pieces with great concentration, and she snips other pages with scissors. Then she pastes the scraps on a piece of construction paper. She loves the creative process and is satisfied with her three-dimensional creation.

If you make a few simple adjustments, children who are physically challenged can also have fun with art experiences.

> **Ivan** found some egg-shaped markers that have caps with animals on them. They are the perfect size for Gena (30 months) to grasp and use. She can even grasp the cap and get it on and off the marker. When Ivan brought them out for Gena, other children gathered and wanted to play with "Gena's markers." Gena became the focal point of a play activity in which she could participate fully with her classmates. Ivan also used these markers to talk about colors, different animals, and animal sounds.

Enjoy your interactions with twos as they explore and experiment with art materials.

- Describe the child's actions: *First you rolled out the dough. Then you pounded it flat. Now I see you are making circles in the dough by using the paper towel roll.*
- Talk about the sensory experience the child is having: *When your fingers move through that Goop, does it feel slippery?*
- Ask open-ended questions: *How did you make those wavy lines in the finger paint?*
- Encourage problem solving: *How can you keep the paint from dripping down the paper on the easel?*

Your interest in what a child is doing makes any experience, including art, both more enjoyable and an opportunity for the child to learn.

Inappropriate Art Activities

Any art activity that focuses on a finished product rather than on the creative process is inappropriate for infants, toddlers, and twos. Young children are not yet developmentally able to create representative art. The following experiences would therefore *not* be part of a developmentally appropriate art program for children under age 3:

- using coloring books
- providing patterns or models for children to copy
- activities where teachers do most of the work (e.g., cutting, taping, stapling, drawing)
- telling a child what to draw, paint, or make
- expecting that a child will produce something recognizable
- "finishing" a child's work to make it "better"

Always keep in mind that, for very young children, art is a sensorimotor experience that builds a foundation for creativity and an appreciation of beauty. The process is more important than what is produced.

Responding to and Planning for Each Child

As you observe children during art experiences, think about the objectives for development and learning. Consider what each child is learning and how you might respond. Here is how four teachers who are implementing *The Creative Curriculum*® use what they learn from their observations to respond to each child and to plan.

Observe	Reflect	Respond
Julio (4 months) nestles into Linda's shoulder, rubbing his cheek on her soft sweater. He smiles and lays his head and hand on her shoulder, patting the sweater.	Julio recognizes and reaches out to a familiar adult (*Objective 2, Establishes and sustains positive relationships; Dimension a, Forms relationships with adults*). He is exploring an object, using his senses (*Objective 11, Demonstrates positive approaches to learning; Dimension d, Shows curiosity and motivation*).	Linda talks to Julio in soothing tones to help build a trusting relationship with him. She comments on what he is doing, "Feel how warm and fuzzy the sweater is, Julio."
Willard (11 months) dips his fingers into paint and begins to push his finger across the paper in the tray. He makes a few small marks, dips his fingers in again, and makes a few more. He smiles, dips his whole hand in, and smears it across the entire paper.	Willard is learning how objects work by handling them (*Objective 11, Demonstrates positive approaches to learning; Dimension d, Shows curiosity and motivation*). He is noticing particular characteristics of objects (*Objective 26, Demonstrates knowledge of the physical properties of objects and materials*).	Grace encourages his exploration of the paint and says, "Willard you covered your whole paper." She points to a blank sheet of paper and asks, "Would you like to paint another?"

Observe	Reflect	Respond
Matthew (22 months) holds a marker in each hand, scribbling up and down on a large piece paper. He looks at Jenna (24 months), who is also drawing with markers. Then he reaches over and draws a line across her paper. Jenna scowls. Matthew quickly pulls his hand away.	Matthew is showing awareness that others' feelings are separate from his own feelings (*Objective 2, Establishes and sustains positive relationships*; *Dimension b, Responds to emotional cues*). He is experimenting with scribbling (*Objective 7, Demonstrates fine-motor strength*; *Dimension b, Uses writing and drawing tools*).	To support Matthew's understanding of others' feelings, Mercedes explains, "Jenna didn't like it when you wrote on her paper. She made an angry face, and you stopped." "Here is your paper, Matthew," she says as she points to his paper. "You can make lots of lines on this one."
While playing outside, Valisha (33 months) picks up a piece of stubby chalk and begins scribbling on the blacktop. She tells LaToya, "I drawing hopscotch."	Valisha is scribbling with the intention of communicating (*Objective 19, Demonstrates emergent writing skills*; *Dimension b, Writes to convey meaning*). She is coordinating her eye and hand movements to complete increasingly complicated tasks (*Objective 7, Demonstrates fine-motor strength and coordination*; *Dimension a, Uses fingers and hands*)	To promote Valisha's positive feelings about her writing, LaToya says, "Oh, I see that you are drawing a hopscotch board with that chalk. We can play hopscotch when you are finished?"

Responsive Planning

In developing weekly plans, these teachers use their observations and refer to *Objectives for Development & Learning*. Here is what they record on their weekly planning forms.

- As Linda reads her observation notes, she realizes that a couple of the children have been interested in fabric textures. She decides that she will bring fabric swatches with different textures to put out for the children to explore on Wednesday, Thursday, and Friday. She records this on the "Group Planning Form." Under "Family Involvement," she makes a note to ask families on Monday to bring in any fabric that they are willing to donate.

- On the "Child Planning Form," under "Current Information," Grace writes a brief note about Willard's experience with finger paint. Under "Plans," she notes that she will offer finger painting again the following week but provide larger sheets of paper for him to experiment on.

- On the "Child Planning Form," under "Current Information," Mercedes writes about Matthew's interaction with Jenna. Under "Plans," she writes that she will set up a group art activity so Matthew has the opportunity to share an art experience with his peers. On the "Group Planning Form," under "Wednesday," she records that she will bring a large sheet of butcher paper to the playground for the children to paint a group mural.

- LaToya records her observation of Valisha on the "Child Planning Form." Under "Plans," she writes a note to add some more writing tools to the art area. On the "Group Planning Form," under "Changes to the Environment," she makes a list of the writing materials she will add. She also writes, under "Monday," that she will introduce small chalk boards and stubby chalk as an indoor experience for the children to explore all week.

With your support and interactions, young children learn and grow through art experiences. You can also help families appreciate all of the learning that occurs through art. On the following page, you will find a letter that you can send home to families explaining the role that art plays in your program.

Dear Families:

When you think about art experiences, do you imagine a child with crayons or a paint brush in hand? Painting and drawing are just two of the many ways young children enjoy art. In fact, art experiences begin early in life as a baby enjoys stroking the fringe on her blanket or finger paints with the blob of yogurt that falls on her tray. As they get older, they enjoy scribbling with a crayon and squeezing playdough with their hands. Art experiences allow children to have wonderful sensory experiences and to experiment with a variety of materials. They also help children develop thinking and physical skills. Here are some examples.

When your child does this...	Your child is learning...
• covers paper with paint	• about cause and effect
• pokes a hole in playdough	• how objects can be used
• tears paper for a collage	• eye-hand coordination
• uses paste successfully	• to solve a problem

What You Can Do at Home

Young children like to explore and experiment with art materials. They are more interested in feeling, seeing, smelling, tasting, and controlling tools and materials than in making something. Here are some ideas for offering art experiences at home.

- **Offer your baby different textures to explore.** Place a basket with a collection of different fabrics near your child and encourage her to play with them. Talk about how they feel.

- **Make simple art materials together.** You can make playdough for your child to squeeze and pound, or make Goop for another wonderful sensory experience. We have several recipes for making art materials that we'll be glad to share with you.

- **Keep plain paper and crayons available for your toddler.** Encourage your child to draw freely and to experiment. Do not expect her to draw something you will be able to recognize.

- **Encourage your child to use art materials freely.** For young children, the process of creating is important, not the finished product. Show your interest in what your child is doing by describing his actions: "You made lots of different marks on the paper. These are round circles, and these are lines."

Together, we can give your child the kinds of experiences that encourage exploration and an appreciation of art.

Sincerely,

16

Tasting and Preparing Food

Supporting Development and Learning 338

**Creating an Environment for
Tasting and Preparing Foods   339**
Selecting Materials for Different Ages   339
Selecting and Displaying Materials   340
Keeping Children Safe and Heathy   341

Caring and Teaching   342
Responding to and Planning for Each Child   346

**Sharing Thoughts About
Tasting and Preparing Food   349**

Tasting and Preparing Food

LaToya tells the children in her group, "We have an exciting snack today. We have carrots right from our garden! After we scrub them, we can taste the vegetable we grew." LaToya asks Valisha (33 months) to help her set vegetable brushes and water bowls on the trays in front of the children. She then hands each child two carrots to scrub. As Jonisha (33 months) displays her washed carrot for the other children to see, LaToya exclaims, "I don't think it could be any cleaner!"

When you invite children to taste and otherwise explore a new food or include them in helping you prepare a snack, you are promoting more than good nutrition. Food and related conversation and activities encourage development and learning in all areas. They evoke feelings of security because children associate them with family and home. They also provide a wealth of sensory experiences and promote the development of fine-motor, cognitive, and language skills.

Tasting and preparing food are part of everyday living with infants, toddlers, and twos. Children become aware of the tastes and textures of various cereals, fruits, and vegetables as you and their families gradually introduce new foods. They begin to express their personal preferences and start to learn the names of different foods. At first, they are primarily interested in squishing, mashing, and smearing food. Before long, they become eager and able to help prepare some of the foods they eat, especially because they like to participate in activities that are important to adults. Whether it is scrubbing a carrot or dipping a slice of apple in melted cheese, children enjoy and are proud to help you with meaningful tasks.

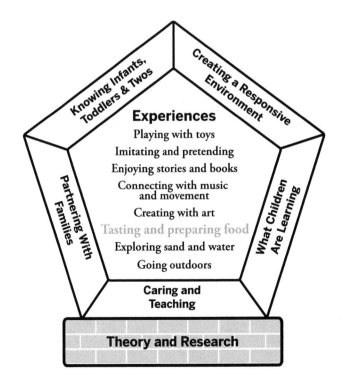

Supporting Development and Learning

While they are tasting and preparing food, children have opportunities to strengthen their social–emotional, physical, cognitive, and language skills.

Learning about themselves and others: Infants are eager to practice the skills that enable them to feed themselves. Toddlers and twos learn to work cooperatively with others in preparing simple foods. They also develop other personal care skills, such as washing their hands, serving themselves, and cleaning up after themselves.

Learning about moving: Children strengthen their small muscles by such activities as tearing lettuce for a salad and scrubbing vegetables. They coordinate their eye-hand movements when they pour water into a cup or spread apple butter on a cracker. Their whole bodies are involved as they help with cleanup, sweep the floor with a child-sized broom, or walk to the trash can with a banana peel in hand.

Learning about the world: Children build a foundation for mathematical thinking when they sort fruit by color and fill a quart pitcher with cups of water. They learn problem-solving skills when they fill a muffin tin only halfway so the batter does not overflow as it bakes. They observe scientific principles as they shake cream until butter forms and as they watch cheese melt. They learn how objects are used when they mix pancake batter with a wooden spoon, help you spoon muffin batter into pans, and experiment with using a rubber spatula.

Learning about communicating: Children learn the vocabulary of cooking when they *knead* dough, *chop* pieces of fruit, and *stir* pancake batter. As twos follow simple picture and word recipes, they learn that pictures and print convey messages. They also learn to follow simple directions and to have conversations with children and adults.

Creating an Environment for Tasting and Preparing Foods

Food experiences are best when they take place near a sink, because then cleanup goes more smoothly. If you are going to use an electrical appliance, make sure your space includes an outlet where you can plug it in safely. A washable floor makes it easier to clean up the inevitable spills.

Selecting Materials for Different Ages

Young Infants

Most food experiences for young infants are seeing, tasting, smelling, and touching experiences, so you don't need to do anything special. They only need their eyes, mouths, noses, and hands. A teaspoon of rice cereal for a 4- to 6-month-old is a new taste and texture sensation. By 8 or 9 months, a young infant and you can take turns directing food to his mouth. You might wish to give an infant a cracker to hold and nibble between the bites of cottage cheese that you spoon into her mouth.

Mobile Infants

Spoons, training cups, and new foods are interesting challenges for mobile infants. They can also begin to participate in food preparation activities. Wooden spoons, plastic mixing bowls, and rubber spatulas are important tools for this age-group.

Toddlers and Twos

Toddlers and twos can participate more fully in food preparation activities. Provide utensils that children can use on their own. As much as possible, offer children real utensils rather than toy ones. Real gadgets and utensils not only make the experience more authentic, but they are less frustrating to use than toys that are not intended to work. Utensils that toddlers and twos can learn to use include mixing spoons and spatulas, plastic measuring cups, vegetable brushes, wire whisks, and potato mashers.

You can help children who have physical disabilities participate in cooking activities by providing adapted cups, utensils, and dishes. Suction cups provide a stable base for both eating and mixing bowls. Rubberized nonslip material can also be used under utensils and bowls to prevent sliding. Ask the child's parents for suggestions about what adaptations work well. Adaptive aids can sometimes be found at hardware and kitchen stores, and specialty items are sold at medical supply outlets that carry aids for daily living.

With your supervision, twos can prepare simple snacks. You can make simple picture recipe cards that show the steps. Recipe cards not only teach children about following directions, they also help children learn that pictures and print carry meaning.

Selecting and Displaying Materials

Here are some considerations for planning food-related experiences.

Think about the equipment you will need. For example, if an oven is not available, a toaster oven or a wok might do nicely.

Provide a child-sized table and chairs. To enjoy food preparation experiences fully, children need to be able to work, move about, and observe freely. A child-size table can be used as a work station as well as for eating. Chairs enable children to sit while they observe, thereby minimizing children's getting in each other's way.

Store safe cooking tools and utensils in low cabinets. If materials are stored on low shelves, the older children can get what they need on their own. Picture and word labels show toddlers and twos where these materials belong, so they can find what they need and help clean up.

Provide smocks. When their clothing is protected, you do not have to worry about stains and the children can participate fully. If you do not have smocks, you or a parent can easily make them from old shirts or pieces of oilcloth.

Store nontoxic cleanup supplies where you can reach them easily. Invite children to help you wipe up the spills that are sure to occur.

Keeping Children Safe and Heathy

Pay careful attention to food safety when planning food experiences. Refrigerate all perishable foods, especially milk, milk products, eggs, and mayonnaise. Do not leave them out of the refrigerator for more than an hour. Before and after handling food, wash your and the children's hands well. Help children remember not to return their tasting spoons to a common bowl.

Food preparation experiences that involve using real utensils, tools, and appliances require close supervision. Preventive measures will eliminate many potential problems. For example, by choosing nonbreakable materials, you guard against injuries. Storing adult items, such as egg beaters and electrical appliances, out of children's reach or in a locked cupboard also minimizes injuries.

Before beginning food experiences with children, it is vitally important to know whether any children have food allergies. Many young children are allergic to egg whites, soy, wheat, and peanuts. Children who are lactose intolerant have to avoid milk and milk products such as yogurt and ice cream. Ask parents about food allergies when you complete the "Individual Care Plan—Family Information Form." Not only do you want to keep children from eating anything that might harm them, you want to plan food-related learning experiences in which children are able to participate fully.

Before children begin to prepare food, you need to talk with them about basic safety rules. Consult your local health department for the latest health and safety information. Helpful resources are available from the United States Department of Health and Human Services' Maternal and Child Health Bureau and from the Department of Agriculture's Food and Nutrition Services.

During any tasting and food preparation experience with children, there is always the possibility that, despite every precaution, a child might gag or choke. Because it is often difficult to think clearly in an emergency, it makes good sense to post the first-aid guidelines for choking in the area where you will be providing food experiences. Make sure your first-aid and CPR training and certification are current.

Caring and Teaching

As you offer children food tasting and preparation experiences, think about what they are learning. Observe children as they try a new food or help you peel an orange for a snack, and note how they are mastering physical, cognitive, social–emotional, and language skills.

Young Infants

Food experiences for young infants involve both tasting foods and building relationships with those who feed them. When you hold an infant and feed him his bottle, he tastes the milk, gets nutrients, and, equally important, he feels safe and secure.

> **Janet** gives Jasmine (8 months) opportunities to explore her food, and she talks with Jasmine about what is happening. She also takes advantage of opportunities to introduce the names of foods, adjectives that describe them, and verbs that explain what the child is doing.
>
> When Jasmine tries to pick up applesauce with her fist, Janet comments, "You're having a hard time picking up the applesauce. It is very slippery." When Jasmine pounds a slice of banana with her fist, Janet asks, "You like mashing that squishy banana, don't you?"

Mobile Infants

In addition to food-tasting experiences, mobile infants enjoy being involved in the preparation of their snacks. Food experiences for children of this age involve shaking, dabbing, dipping, stirring, and mashing. Here are some examples of appropriate learning experiences:

- shaking grated cheese on macaroni or vegetable purees (squash, green beans, peas, carrots, beets, cauliflower, or zucchini)
- dropping cheese cubes onto rice or mashed potatoes
- dabbing apple butter on bread or toast
- shaking cinnamon on cottage cheese, yogurt, cooked cereal, or applesauce
- dipping banana chunks, steamed apple, or pear wedges into yogurt
- mixing cottage cheese with macaroni, kasha (roasted buckwheat), or bow-tie pasta
- making dips for snacks by mixing grated cheese or spices (such as powdered cinnamon and nutmeg) with sour cream, yogurt, or mashed chick peas

As you help mobile infants prepare food, observe them carefully so you will know how to respond. Stretch children's thinking as you interact with them.

- Encourage vocabulary development by modeling complete language: *We're going to use the avocado to make a dip called* guacamole.
- Encourage children to think about cause and effect: *Let's see what happens to the avocado when we mash it.*
- Promote children's understanding of how objects can be used: *Abby, will you please hand me the potato masher so that we can mash the avocado? Come here, and I'll show you how it works.*

Toddlers and Twos

Toddlers and especially twos can take an even more active role in preparing foods. On the basis of the children's interests and abilities, you can plan activities that involve spreading, pouring, slicing, whisking, squeezing, and garnishing. Here are typical favorites:

- preparing finger foods by topping cucumber slices, toast strips, or crackers with cheese, cottage cheese, or fruit wedges

- using a plastic knife or a small icing spatula to spread fruit butter on crackers, bread, or toast

- stirring together the ingredients for hot cereal, and pouring milk or maple syrup into the bowl

- whisking eggs in a bowl

- dipping bread slices in beaten eggs, cinnamon, and milk to make French toast

- scrubbing raw potatoes or yams; mashing cooked potatoes or yams

- mixing gelatin in water; cutting shapes from firm gelatin

- squeezing lemons, oranges, and limes for fruit drinks

- snapping the ends of green beans

- shelling peas

- arranging food decoratively on a plate, tray, or table

As children help prepare food, encourage them to think about what they are doing. Here are some suggestions:

- Describe what you see them doing: *You are using the masher to mash the yams, Gena.*
- Encourage children to think about the effects of their actions: *How do the mashed yams look different from the whole yams? Is it easier to eat mashed yams or whole yams?*

Observe the children in your care to see what skills they are developing. Then use the information to plan experiences that will extend their learning.

Jonisha (33 months), like several of the other children, enjoys helping prepare her own morning snack. Knowing this, LaToya prepared recipe cards for banana dip. The first card shows a banana being broken into pieces. The second card shows cinnamon being sprinkled into a bowl of plain yogurt. The third card shows a hand dipping a banana chunk into the dip. LaToya shows the cards to Jonisha, explaining each step. When they finish, she tells Jonisha, "I'm going to sit next to you as you make banana dip for your snack. If you need any help, I'm right here." Jonisha smiles broadly as LaToya moves the plate of peeled bananas closer to her.

LaToya made sure that Jonisha had a successful experience by thinking about what needed to be done ahead of time. She peeled the bananas and set out all of the ingredients. She made and reviewed the recipe cards with Jonisha before the child tried to make her snack. She stayed nearby to lend support. While Jonisha made the dip, LaToya described what Jonisha was doing and commented on how it was just what the recipe cards said to do.

To extend the learning experience, LaToya later brought out some other fruits (apple slices and a strawberry) and some vegetables (carrot sticks and seedless cucumber slices). Then she asked Jonisha to try them and to think about the different tastes. Jonisha did not much like the carrot or cucumber, but she was very happy to eat the fruits. Encouraged by LaToya's questions, Jonisha concluded that fruits are better for dipping than vegetables.

In order to document this learning experience, LaToya photographed the activity. She then put copies of the photos in a homemade book and noted what Jonisha is doing in each picture. By doing this, she will enable Jonisha's parents to see what their daughter has been learning. She knows that Jonisha will love looking at the book *Jonisha Dips a Banana*.

As you begin to plan food preparation activities, start with the snacks you serve to the children. Think about how you might involve the children in preparing them. Choose recipes that have a limited number of steps and require only beginning physical skills, such as dipping, shaking, or mashing. More complex skills, such as pouring, spreading, and squeezing, can be added as children's mastery of fine-motor skills improves.

For special projects, you might want to consult some of the published books for preparing foods that toddlers like. Simplify recipes that you think children will enjoy into two or three steps. Then make picture and word recipe cards that illustrate the steps.

Although there are a number of excellent cookbooks for young children that make use of recipe cards, most will be too complicated for your needs. These books are more appropriate for use with preschoolers and older children, even if they claim to be for infants, toddlers, and twos. Others include the preparation of foods that are nutritionally inappropriate. To use cookbooks effectively with infants, toddlers, and twos, you will need to rethink the recipes in terms of children's skills and special dietary requirements.

Families are another good resource for cooking ideas. Invite parents to share recipes for foods they prepare for their children at home. By preparing and serving these foods at your program, you strengthen the bond between home and the program. Including family recipes is one way for your program to acknowledge the backgrounds of the children and families you serve.

Responding to and Planning for Each Child

As you observe children during tasting and food preparation experiences, think about the objectives for development and learning. Consider what each child is learning and how you might respond. Here is how four teachers who are implementing *The Creative Curriculum®* use what they learn from their observations to respond to each child and to plan.

Observe	Reflect	Respond
Jasmine (8 months) drinks from a cup as Janet holds it for her at snack time. She lifts her hands and bangs the sides of the cup.	Jasmine is attempting a simple personal care task (*Objective 1, Regulates own emotions and behaviors*; Dimension c, *Takes care of own needs appropriately*).	Janet describes what Jasmine is doing, "You are drinking from the cup." Then she asks, "Would you like to hold the cup?"
Abby (14 months) sits at the table when she sees Brooks setting it for snack.	Abby is expecting to participate in group routines (*Objective 1, Regulates own emotions and behaviors*; Dimension b, *Follows limits and expectations*).	Brooks says, "Abby, you know it is time to eat snack because you see me putting out the bowls." She holds her hand out to Abby and says, "Let's go wash our hands so we may eat."
Matthew (22 months) is helping to make pancakes for breakfast. He pours milk from a small pitcher into the mixing bowl, spilling some on the table. He exclaims, "Uh-oh!" and gets a wipe to clean the table.	Matthew is using eye-hand coordination while doing simple tasks (*Objective 7, Demonstrates fine-motor strength*; Dimension a, *Uses fingers and hands*). He is planning ways to use objects to perform one-step tasks (*Objective 11, Demonstrates positive approaches to learning*; Dimension e, *Shows flexibility and inventiveness in thinking*).	"Accidents happen," Mercedes says. "Thank you for cleaning it up so quickly. Give it another try! We still need milk in the bowl."

Observe	Reflect	Respond
Valisha (33 months) pulls LaToya toward the toaster oven. She smells muffins baking and says, "Muffins are ready. I'm hungry."	Valisha is carrying out her own plan for solving a problem *(Objective 11, Demonstrates positive approaches to learning; Dimension c, Solves problems).* She is using simple sentences with three or more words *(Objective 9, Uses language to express thoughts and needs; Dimension c, Uses conventional grammar).*	LaToya acknowledges Valisha's presence and interest by saying, "I smell those muffins, too. You are hungry and ready to eat them. They are almost done baking." To encourage Valisha's problem-solving skills, she asks, "What should we do to get the table ready for snack time?"

Responsive Planning

In developing weekly plans, these teachers use their observations and refer to *Objectives for Development & Learning*. Here is what they record on their weekly planning forms.

- On the *"Child Planning Form,"* under "Current Information," Janet writes that Jasmine is beginning to be interested in feeding herself. Under "Plans," she notes that she will offer Jasmine more opportunities to feed herself finger foods and that she will offer her a spill-proof cup. Janet also makes a note about this on the *"Group Planning Form,"* under "Changes to Routines."

- After reviewing her observation notes, Brooks realizes that a few of the children are beginning to participate in mealtimes as a group. She decides that she will take photographs of the children as they prepare for mealtimes and create a book that she can share with them and that illustrates the steps of the routine. On her *"Group Planning Form,"* under "Indoor Experiences" for Monday, Tuesday, and Wednesday, she writes that she will share the book with the children.

- On the *"Child Planning Form,"* under "Current Information," Mercedes records Matthew's interest in cooking and his increasing eye-hand coordination. Under "Plans," she notes that she will add small pitchers and bowls to the water table and that she will offer two food preparation experiences next week. On the *"Group Planning Form,"* under "Indoor Experiences," she records her plan for the children to help prepare their snacks on Tuesday (cut vegetables and yogurt dip) and Thursday (pear bunnies).

- LaToya records Valisha's interest in preparing food on the *"Child Planning Form."* Under "Plans" she writes that she will make pancakes with the children next week.

Tasting and preparing foods is a good way to promote development in all areas. The letter to families is a way to offer ideas about sharing food-related experiences with their children.

Dear Families:

Perhaps the idea of involving very young children in food preparation seems strange to you. However, one of the reasons that preparing food appeals to children is that it is a meaningful, grown-up activity. Participating in activities that your child observes you doing every day is exciting for them.

In our program, we build on the children's interest in food experiences because they help your child develop many concepts and skills. For example, what do you think your child might learn from a simple task such as snapping the ends off green beans? Did you think about these concepts and skills?

- shape
- color
- part and whole
- cause and effect

- sustaining attention
- eye-hand coordination
- fine-motor skills

As you can see, preparing food is educational as well as practical and fun!

What You Can Do at Home

At home, children can be involved easily in food preparation. Here are some ideas.

- **Let your child help.** Because you probably already cook at home, it's easy for you to involve your child. You can even include a young infant. Let her sit where she can watch you as you describe what you are doing. Older infants, toddlers, and twos can participate more actively. When you let your child help you prepare and serve foods, you show that you value his contributions to family life.

- **Talk about the foods and what each of you is doing.** Here are some topics to discuss as you prepare and taste foods together:
  - the names of different foods and how they look, smell, feel, taste, and sometimes sound
  - what different utensils are used for and where you keep them
  - why you serve a variety of foods with each meal

Maybe you'd like to help the children cook at our program. We'd love for you to supply a recipe or help the children make their snack. Also, please send us your ideas for food preparation experiences. We especially welcome your family favorites. We want your child to have wonderful food-related experiences both here and at home.

Sincerely,

17

Exploring Sand and Water

Supporting Development and Learning 352

**Creating an Environment for
Sand and Water Play** 353
Selecting Materials for Different Ages 354
Setting Up and Displaying Materials 355

Caring and Teaching 356
Responding to and Planning for Each Child 361

**Sharing Thoughts About
Exploring Sand and Water** 363

Exploring Sand and Water

Willard (11 months) waves the rubber animal he has just washed. "That has to be the cleanest dinosaur I've ever seen! Look how shiny it is when it's wet," Grace exclaims. Willard babbles in reply and flashes a smile as he hands the dinosaur to her. He turns around and points at the shelf with the other rubber animals. "I bet you want to wash another animal," Grace prompts. "How about this giraffe? He really needs a bath."

Sand and water are readily available and provide wonderful sensory experiences. There is something about the cool water and the sensation of sand sifting through fingers that almost everyone finds appealing. Sand and water are soothing materials that can calm children and keep them happily engaged.

Most young infants thoroughly enjoy simple water play. Being held by someone they love and the effects they get by kicking and slapping the water are satisfying experiences. Adding a few props, such as cups and rubber animals, can extend the play of mobile infants for long periods of time. Sand and water play are usually among the favorite activities of toddlers and twos, who purposefully explore and experiment with tools and other objects.

Sand and water play can take place outdoors or indoors. It all depends on the weather and your setup.

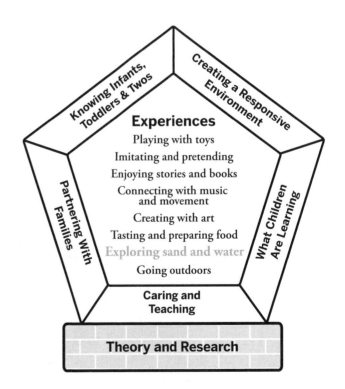

Supporting Development and Learning

Children develop social–emotional, physical, cognitive, and language skills as they play with sand and water. Here are some examples.

Learning about themselves and others: When you interact with children as they play with sand and water, they use their trust in you as a secure base from which to explore the materials. Playing near other children, they take an interest in what others are doing and start to imitate their actions. If there are plenty of props for everyone, children will be more likely to start playing together.

Learning about moving: Children strengthen their hand muscles and improve eye-hand coordination when they scoop and sift sand, pour water or sand from one container to another, and squeeze water from a baster. They build large muscles when they chase bubbles and carry a bucket of sand from one side of the yard to another. Eye-hand coordination also improves as they practice using simple tools.

Learning about the world: Children make exciting discoveries as they experiment with sand and water. They find out that they can hide things in sand but not in water. They see how sand moves when it is sifted, raked, and shoveled, and how water can be poured and splashed. They learn that sand and water can be stored in containers. Playing with sand and water offers many opportunities to learn about cause and effect and to solve problems.

Learning about communicating: As adults model relevant language, children learn to describe their experiences. As children experiment with sand and water, they ask and answer questions during their play. Sand and water also support the development of pretend play that involves increasingly complex conversation.

Creating an Environment for Sand and Water Play

Because sand and water play are somewhat messy, prepare your environment in advance. If you are not worried about spills, the children will be free to explore and have fun. An uncarpeted area is the logical choice. If this is not available, protect carpeted floors by spreading a plastic tablecloth, shower curtain, or tarp on the floor. To make cleaning up spilled water even easier, spread old towels on top of the plastic.

As always, children's health and safety is a primary consideration. You will need to review and follow the health and safety standards that apply to sand and water.

Keeping Children Safe and Healthy

- Supervise children who are playing with sand and water closely. Be ready to step in to prevent injuries.

- Teach toddlers and twos a few simple rules, such as "Keep the water in the basin."

- Use individual trays or tubs to reduce the spread of germs.

- Use only fresh water in water tubs and empty the tubs after each use. Standing water is a drowning hazard and an ideal environment for bacteria to grow.

- Sanitize water tubs and props after each use, using a mild bleach solution of 1 tablespoon of liquid chlorine bleach to 1 gallon of water or 1 teaspoon of liquid chlorine bleach to 1 quart of water.

- Cover outdoor sandboxes when they are not in use, to keep animals out of them.

Selecting Materials for Different Ages

Sand and water are satisfying materials for very young children. As children develop, they also discover the fun and possibilities that props and toys add to their play.

Young Infants

Sand is not recommended for young infants because they put it in their mouths. Instead, begin with water play. Feeling and splashing water usually delight young infants. Once they can sit on their own, a small basin with about an inch of water and a few very simple props like plastic cups and rubber toys will keep them engaged.

Mobile Infants

Both sand and water play are appropriate for mobile infants. Their play is likely to involve filling and dumping cups and pails. When you add floating toys for water play and various scoops for sand play, children discover what they can do with them. Each discovery is a wonderful surprise.

Toddlers and Twos

By age 2, children become more purposeful in their explorations of sand and water. In addition to the props you provide for mobile infants, gradually introduce more that will inspire toddlers and twos to experiment and pretend. Here are some suggestions for additional props:

- plastic or rubber animals, people, boats, and other vehicles
- wire whisks
- rakes and shovels
- small watering cans
- sieves
- water/sand mills
- plastic cookie cutters
- slotted spoons
- squeeze bottles, basters

- pie tins (with and without bottom holes)
- ladles
- scoops
- muffin tins
- straws
- bubble-blowing solution and supplies
- collectibles that are not choking hazards, such as large shells, feathers, and pinecones

Setting Up and Displaying Materials

When you offer **water play** to infants, begin with no more than a cafeteria tray of water. As children become more mobile, you can use a plastic basin with 2–3 inches of water. Toddlers and twos can use a water table of an appropriate height. A table on wheels can be pushed outside on warm days. Consider placing individual basins inside the water table, to limit the spread of germs and give each child a defined space in which to play.

For **sand play**, sterilized, fine-grained sand (sold at hardware and home improvement stores) is best for health reasons. A sand table works well for older infants, toddlers, and twos. You can put a small amount of sand in individual basins to be used on a table or inside a large sand table. When using individual basins, pick smaller props such as coffee scoops, small rakes, funnels, plastic animals, and vehicles.

Props for sand and water play should be kept where children can reach them easily. Make sure that they are attractively displayed and readily visible, so children can find what they want to use. Here are some ideas for displaying materials.

Place props at children's eye level so they can see what is available.

Use baskets or plastic boxes to hold collectibles such as shells.

Store props in baskets or plastic containers by function. For example, one basket might have props for filling, such as scoops, measuring cups, and shovels. Another basket might have props for making bubbles, including bubble solution, wands, straws, and homemade bubble frames.

Tape a picture and word label on the outside of the container and on the shelf where it is kept. Cover the labels with clear contact paper or tape, to protect them from wet fingers.

Caring and Teaching

Observe and talk with children as they play with sand and water, and show them how delighted you are with their discoveries. You will learn a lot about each child's temperament, interests, and developing skills. Then you can use what you learn from your observations to plan ways to extend their learning.

Young Infants

Your positive relationships with young infants provide a secure base from which they can explore new materials and sensations.

> **Julio** (4 months) sits in Linda's lap while she makes a game of dripping water on his feet. He squeals with delight and presses his back against Linda. As Linda observes Julio's reaction, she is happy to see how comfortable Julio is with her. Julio now trusts her to keep him safe and help him manage new sensations. She sees water play as an opportunity to build their relationship by sharing an enjoyable experience.

Babies who are a bit older enjoy making their own discoveries. They can play more independently.

> **Jasmine** (8 months), is much more active physically than Julio. Rather than sit on Janet's lap during water play, she likes to sit on the floor and conduct her own experiments with water. She especially likes to pat and slap the shallow tray of water that Janet places near her.

As you help young infants play with water, talk about what they are experiencing and doing.

- Describe the child's reaction: *That water felt cool on your skin. It surprised you, didn't it?*
- Talk about what a child does: *You slapped the water with your hand, so it splashed.*
- Sing about water-related activities: *Row, row, row your boat...*

Mobile Infants

By the time they are mobile infants, children explore sand and water more intentionally. They like to use their hands as tools, and simple props enhance their play. Filling and emptying containers with sand or water are satisfying for them. As they play, mobile infants develop eye-hand coordination and begin to learn about cause and effect, and about the properties of sand, water, containers, and other props.

Abby (14 months) discovers that water and sand feel different, and she begins to understand the meaning of wet and dry. She finds out that sand changes when it is combined with water. Brooks makes a habit of introducing new vocabulary to Abby during sand and water play. She uses new words as she converses with Abby: "Look. The wet sand is darker than the dry sand, and it sticks together when you pat it."

Here are some ways to promote the learning of mobile infants as they play with sand and water.

- Describe changes the child can observe: *The sand became wet and dark when we added water.*

- Encourage children to appreciate designs: *You made wavy lines in the sand with the rake.*

- Help children become aware of their feelings: *Playing with water is so much fun!*

- Talk about what you and the child are doing: *I'm going to dip the wand in the bubble solution. Let's see what happens when you blow on it.*

Toddlers and Twos

Most toddlers begin applying what they have learned about the properties of sand and water. For example, instead of simply scooping wet sand in and out of pails, they now use tools to mold shapes. They are still experimenting, however. They want to see what will happen when they deliberately do something with these materials, and they predict the effects of their actions. Children also begin to engage in pretend play as they explore sand and water.

> **Leo** (18 months) pushes a toy boat through a basin of water, saying, "Toot, toot."
>
> **Jonisha** (33 months) tells LaToya, "Need more water." Then she pours a little water into a pail of sand, turns the pail over, and announces, "I made a house."

When they have many opportunities to explore sand and water and to use different props, children discover that some objects float on water but some sink, and that sifted sand forms a mound. They enjoy filling a bucket with damp sand, turning it over to make a cake, and then smashing it. They will do this repeatedly, just as they love to build towers with blocks, knock them down, and build them again.

To promote their learning during sand and water play, talk with toddlers and twos about what they are doing. Here are some examples:

- Point out cause-and-effect relationships: *What happened to the sand when you poured it in the colander?*
- Encourage children to solve problems: *How can you get this sand into the bucket?*
- Encourage children to make predictions: *What will happen if you drop the block in the water?*
- Support pretend play: *Your baby doll is getting nice and clean because you are giving her a bath. I think she's going to be hungry when you finish bathing her. Do you have some food for her?*

Props help 2-year-olds explore sand and water in new ways. As they experiment, twos learn new concepts.

Valisha (33 months) uses a whisk in the water tray after LaToya adds liquid detergent. She makes bubbles that disappear when she pokes them. She sees that sand falls through the colander when it is dry but not when it is wet.

Introduce props gradually, making sure that twos have plenty of time to try them. One all-time favorite for young children is blowing bubbles.

Bubble Solution

2/3 cup of liquid detergent (Joy® or Dawn® work best)

1 quart of water

1/3 cup of glycerin

Dip empty frames into the solution to make large bubbles. To make foamy bubbles, use empty shampoo bottles.

Provide a variety of frames to dip into the bubble solution and then wave or blow on. Empty eyeglass frames and plastic berry baskets make wonderful bubbles. Show children that bubble blowing works best when both their hands and the frames are completely wet. A dry surface often causes bubbles to burst on contact.

Here are other activities you might try with toddlers and twos:

- painting a building, sidewalk, fence, or tree with water
- playing music to set the tone for children's sand and water play
- reading stories about going to the beach and about boats and earth-moving equipment

Get to know children's temperaments, likes, and dislikes so that you can offer appropriate sand and water experiences.

Barbara knows that Leo (18 months) occasionally has emotional outbursts and temper tantrums. She finds that sand and water play calm Leo when he loses control of his emotions. "You may take away our books and balls," says Barbara, "but if you take away our sand and water tubs, Leo and I won't make it through the day."

Responding to and Planning for Each Child

As you observe children playing with sand and water, think about the objectives for development and learning. Consider what each child is learning and how you might respond. Here is how three teachers who are implementing *The Creative Curriculum®* use what they learn from their observations to respond to each child and to plan.

Observe	Reflect	Respond
Jasmine (8 months) holds both of Janet's hands as she takes a few steps around the playground. Jasmine stops to watch two toddlers who are digging in the sandbox.	Jasmine watches and responds to other children (*Objective 2, Establishes and sustains positive relationships*; *Dimension c, Interacts with peers*). She is beginning to gain balance and to move from place to place (*Objective 4, Demonstrates traveling skills*).	Janet sits with Jasmine on the ground near the children who are digging. She talks to Jasmine about what they are doing: "Tyler and Shontelle are having a great time, digging with their shovels."
Willard (11 months) picks up a large plastic snap bead from the sand tray where he has been playing and hands it to Grace.	Willard uses his thumb and index finger to grasp and drop objects (*Objective 7, Demonstrates fine-motor strength*; *Dimension a, Uses fingers and hands*). He continues an activity when an adult interacts (*Objective 11, Demonstrates positive approaches to learning*; *Dimension a, Attends and engages*).	To encourage Willard, Grace smiles at him and says, "Thank you for the bead, Willard. May I have another one?"
Matthew (22 months) tries to take a small toy boat out of the water table by using a wooden spoon. The boat falls off the spoon. He tries again, but the boat falls. He looks around, chooses a small fishnet, and lifts the boat out. He looks at Mercedes and smiles.	Matthew plans ways to use objects to perform one-step tasks (*Objective 11, Demonstrates positive approaches to learning*; *Dimension e, Shows flexibility and inventiveness in thinking*). He persists with trial-and-error approaches to solving a problem (*Objective 11, Demonstrates positive approaches to learning*; *Dimension b, Persists*).	Mercedes acknowledges Matthew's accomplishment, "Matthew, you found a way to get the boat out. You used the net to solve the problem." She challenges him: "What else can you pick up with the fishnet?"

Responsive Planning

In developing weekly plans, these teachers use their observations and refer to *Objectives for Development & Learning.* Here is what they record on their weekly planning forms.

- On the "Child Planning Form," Janet notes Jasmine's interest in watching the other children. Under "Plans," she writes that she will continue to observe Jasmine when she is playing near other children and encourage her engagement with them.

- Grace records Willard's use of the pincer grasp on the "Child Planning Form." She decides that she will bring out a collection of large plastic keys so that he can continue to practice grasping. She records this under "Plans." On the "Group Planning Form," under "Indoor Experiences," Grace also makes a note about offering the keys on Thursday and Friday.

- On the "Group Planning Form," under "Changes to the Environment," Mercedes records that she will add new tools and small toys to the water table. She plans to add two pairs of tongs, a sieve, and a ladle, as well as several small floating fish and ducks. On the "Child Planning Form," under "Current Information," she records Matthew's problem-solving experience. Under "Plans," she writes a note to encourage him to use the new materials at the water table.

Sand and water play provide infants, toddlers, and twos with wonderful opportunities to explore and experiment. Sometimes families are unaware of the many benefits of this type of play, thinking mostly about the potential mess involved. The letter to families is one way to explain how sand and water play contribute to their child's development.

Dear Families:

Sand and water play is messy, no doubt about that. Children love it, though, and they learn a lot from it. When an infant splashes water, he learns that slapping it makes the water move (cause and effect). When a toddler pours a cup of sand into a bucket, she begins to learn about size, shape, and quantity. When a 2-year-old makes a birthday cake with sand and puts sticks in for candles, he is pretending with objects.

In our program, the children play with sand and water both indoors and outdoors. Young infants splash water in a tray. Older infants wash dolls and rubber toys, and they dig and pour sand. Toddlers and twos squirt water with basters, blow bubbles into the breeze, and make designs in sand with combs and molds.

What You Can Do at Home

We encourage you to enjoy sand and water with your child. Of course, close supervision is needed to keep your child safe. Here are some suggestions to consider.

- **Fill a tray or plastic tub with an inch or so of water.** A small amount of water is all your child needs to have fun. Place the tub on the floor, on top of some towels, and then let your child splash! If you have an older infant, toddler, or 2-year-old, also offer plastic measuring cups, squeeze bottles, and perhaps a funnel or a sieve.
- **Talk with your child during bath time.** Ask questions to encourage observation and thinking: "What will happen if you drop your rubber frog in the water?"
- **Fill a dishpan halfway with clean sand.** That way, your child can play with sand both indoors and out. The dishpan will keep the sand contained. To vary the experience, add a shovel, funnel, coffee scoop, and small plastic animals.
- **Pretend with your child.** When you add a few simple props, sand and water are wonderful materials to encourage pretend play. You and your child can have a tea party, drive boats through the water, and build sand castles and tunnels.

One wonderful benefit of sand and water play is that they are both soothing materials. They can calm a child who is having a hard time. This helps you as well. We will be happy to suggest more ideas for sand and water experiences that you can offer at home.

Sincerely,

18

Going Outdoors

Supporting Development and Learning   **366**

**Creating an Environment for
Outdoor Play**   **367**
Keeping Children Safe and Healthy   368
Outdoor Structures   370
Selecting Materials and Experiences for
Different Ages   371
Including All Children   374

Caring and Teaching   **375**
Responding to and Planning for Each Child   379

**Sharing Thoughts About
Going Outdoors**   **381**

Going Outdoors

Ivan walks over to Gena (30 months), who, from her adaptive stroller, is admiring the fat pea pods growing in the wheelbarrow garden. "Those peas have really grown," he says. "We'll be able to eat them soon." Gena nods and says, "Sun. More sun." Ivan responds, "I think you're right, Gena. We need to move our wheelbarrow garden to a sunny spot." Gena watches Ivan move the garden and then turns her attention to some children who are chasing bubbles. Noticing that Gena is now more interested in what the children are doing, Ivan asks, "Do you want to go over and blow bubbles?" Gena smiles and exclaims, "Yes!" Ivan pushes her to join the other children, opens another jar of bubble solution, and holds the wand so Gena can blow. The other children run over to chase the bubbles, and Gena laughs.

The outdoors offers an entirely different environment for children to explore. There are fresh air and weather to experience: sun, clouds, rain, snow, fog, wind, and hot and cold temperatures. Outdoor environments offer more open space in which to run and stretch. There are different landforms and structures to master: hills, boulders, platforms, tires, swings, and slides. There is also wildlife at which to marvel: caterpillars, worms, birds, bugs, and plants.

Infants, toddlers, and twos should go outdoors every day, unless the weather is extreme or the air quality poses a health risk. All young children need natural spaces that encourage sensory, physical, and social exploration. By the time they are mobile, children enjoy such experiences as splashing water and crawling over a path created with blankets, tires, and floor mats. As toddlers and twos, they cannot resist the challenges of running in open space, climbing on low tree stumps, and propelling themselves on riding toys.

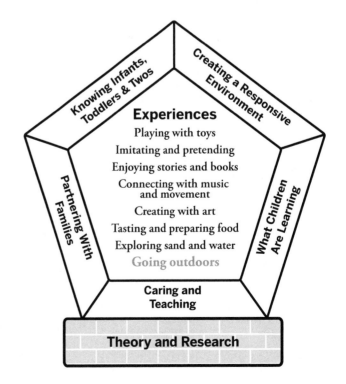

Supporting Development and Learning

Outdoor play can contribute to children's overall development by giving them chances to explore with all of their senses, practice fine and gross-motor skills, develop language and social skills, and begin to appreciate the world around them.

Learning about themselves and others: Depending on the weather, the children might need to put on jackets, hats, mittens and boots before going outside. Dressing and undressing are personal care skills that children develop with practice. Spending time outdoors, especially in natural environments, improves children's mental health and emotional well-being. Children also learn to play with others through such interactions as taking turns with sandbox tools, using the outdoor rocking boat, chasing each other, and pulling each other in a wagon.

Learning about moving: Outdoor play spaces and equipment provide children with many opportunities to build their gross- and fine-motor skills. Lying on a blanket, young infants can move their heads toward the sound of wind chimes, roll over, and reach for streamers. Mobile infants can pull up to standing by holding onto an outdoor cruising rail and take their tentative first steps on a cushion of grass. Toddlers and twos roll, throw, kick, and sometimes manage to catch balls. They walk, run, jump, slide, pedal, and climb. Small muscles get used as children dig and dump in the sandbox, paint the wall with water, or show you the tiny ladybug that they picked up with their thumb and forefinger and carried carefully so they could delight you with their discovery.

Learning about the world: Curious infants, toddlers, and twos investigate and explore the natural world when they play outdoors. They begin to understand cause and effect and make connections. For example, they learn that we wear raincoats when it rains and that the snow melts on warm days. They watch how the wind moves tree branches and listen as birds and airplanes fly overhead. They explore the objects they find outdoors, for example, learning how a shovel can be used in the sandbox and the garden. They notice the differences between dry sand and wet sand. They solve playground problems, such as how to retrieve a ball that rolled under the climber. Sometimes they experiment with more than one solution.

Learning about communicating: There are many outdoor sounds, and children learn to name what they hear. Noticing and discriminating sounds will later be important to the development of literacy skills. Children talk about what they see. Is it a worm, a caterpillar, or a slug? As people converse with them, they learn to describe objects: *fuzzy, fast, shiny, slimy, striped,* and *colorful.* They connect ideas in books, such as reading about fictional animals, with their experiences in the outdoor world, such as finding live animals on the playground.

Creating an Environment for Outdoor Play

To create an interesting and appropriately challenging outdoor space for infants, toddlers, and twos, think about the experiences you want them to have outdoors. Do you remember playing outdoors when you were a child? What appealed to you most? Did you like observing butterflies, catching insects and frogs, watching cloud formations, jumping in piles of leaves, collecting seeds, and building forts? Did you enjoy swinging on swings, moving up and down on a seesaw, climbing to new heights, and throwing and kicking balls?

Recalling your own positive experiences outdoors can help you identify the experiences very young children enjoy outside and how much they benefit from a well-designed environment. Whether your program is urban, suburban, or rural, you can set up interesting structures, offer enjoyable experiences, and help children explore nature.

Keeping Children Safe and Healthy

Ensuring children's safety and health is always a primary consideration. Advanced planning and watchfulness will help you meet the challenges involved in taking children outdoors. Here are some important considerations.

Teacher supervision—Watching and being prepared to intervene when necessary are the primary ways to keep infants, toddlers, and twos safe and healthy outdoors. At all times, you must have enough adults outdoors so that every child is continually supervised.

Conflict prevention—You can reduce hitting, pushing, and biting incidents by offering plenty of interesting things to do. Provide duplicates of favorite outdoor toys such as balls, buckets, shovels, and riding toys. Be alert and ready to step in when necessary.

Developmentally appropriate equipment—Equipment should be designed to match the sizes and skills of infants, toddlers, and twos. A general rule for equipment height is one foot for every year of a child's age (for example, a 2-year-old should use equipment that is no higher than two feet). An average-size adult should not be able to make a structure to wobble or tip. All equipment must meet the standards of the Consumer Product Safety Commission with regard to exposed surfaces, spacing, design, location, and installation.

Layout—The layout of your play area can make it manageable, interesting, and safe. Of course, children who are not yet mobile need to be protected from being bumped by children who are already crawling, walking, and running. Defined areas with clear pathways help control children's traffic and help children choose what to do. Fixed play equipment should be arranged so that the children playing on one piece of equipment will not interfere with children playing on or running to another piece of equipment. To avoid injuries, locate swings and riding toys away from areas where children run.

Shock-absorbent materials—All playground equipment must be surrounded by shock-absorbent material that meets the standards of the Consumer Product Safety Commission. There should be a 6-foot fall zone around the equipment. Shock-absorbent material needs to be raked regularly and checked monthly to determine whether it needs to be replenished. Avoid using rubber and do not use sand if animals are a problem. Also be cautious about using material that children might choke on, such as pea gravel or small wood chips.

Protection from too much sun—In hot weather, sunhats, long-sleeved shirts, and pants provide sun protection. Families must provide sunscreen and written permission for you to use it on their child. Be sure to offer children extra water on hot days. If you do not already have shady places where children can get out of the sun, you can create them. Set up large umbrellas, drape a sheet from a fence, put up a tent, or use an awning.

Nontoxic landscape—Soil should be analyzed for lead content and for other harmful substances when there is reason to believe a problem may exist. Be sure all vegetation is nonpoisonous, in case a curious child takes a taste. Be on the lookout for fire ants, spiders, snakes, and mushrooms, which can sprout up overnight. Check with your regional Poison Control Center or Cooperative Extension Service for complete information.

Water safety—According to the American Academy of Pediatrics and the American Public Health Association, drowning is the third leading cause of the unintentional injury of children younger than age 5.[49] In some states, it is the leading cause of death. To prevent drowning, outside play areas should not include swimming and wading pools, ditches, canals, excavations in which water can collect, fish ponds, and other bodies of water. When providing water play, be sure to empty the containers, because germs collect easily in standing is water. In many areas, standing water is also a breeding site for mosquitoes.

Daily monitoring and maintenance—Outdoor play areas should be checked daily for broken glass, needles, trash, and other hazardous materials such as animal feces, garden chemicals, and paint. Follow your program's procedures for requesting maintenance and repairs.

Monitoring and Maintenance[50]

Check on a regular basis for the following:

- visible cracks, bending, warping, rusting, or breakage of equipment

- faulty or broken hooks, rings, or links

- worn swing hangers and chains

- missing, damaged, or loose swing seats

- broken supports or anchors

- cement support footings that are exposed, cracked, or loose in the ground

- accessible sharp edges or points

- exposed ends of tubing that require caps or plugs

- protruding bolt ends that have lost caps or covers

- loose bolts, nuts, and screws that require tightening

- splintered, cracked, or otherwise deteriorating wood

- lack of lubrication on moving parts

- broken or missing rails, steps, rungs, or seats

- worn or scattered surfacing material

- hard surfaces, especially under swings and slides, where shock-absorbent materials have shifted

- chipped or peeling paint

- pinch or crush points, exposed mechanisms, and moving parts

Outdoor Structures

Some programs have areas with lots of grass, trees, plants, and playground equipment that is designed to match the needs and abilities of children under age 3. Others start with hard ground and very little equipment. Even if your program has few natural materials or structures, there are ways to make it appealing and comfortable for you and the children.

Natural materials—Find nearby places (a farm or gardening center) where you can obtain some bales of hay to put in the yard. If you keep them covered and protected from the rain, they will last a long time. Other natural materials you can bring are low tree stumps, driftwood logs (check for splinters), and large smooth stones. Be sure that the materials are nontoxic.

A garden—You do not need to have a plot of land to have a garden in your play yard. You can make a container garden by filling a wheelbarrow or large pots with rich soil.

Swings—Children can swing on swing sets and with you on a glider. Once infants can sit, you can place them in fully enclosed swings that are high enough off the ground for them to see what is going on nearby. Toddlers and twos can use bucket swings. Swings with a single-strap seat and no back support are not appropriate for children this young.

Slides—A number of companies make sturdy slide structures. Locate them on soft cushioning material. If your outdoor area has a hill, you can embed a slide in the ground, thereby making it safe for even very young children. Check a metal slide each time you take children outdoors on a sunny day, to be sure that it is not too hot.

Platforms and climbers—Climbers do not need to be higher than 18 inches from the ground, and cushioning material should be placed underneath and around them. Low, wide steps or a ramp can lead to a platform that is large enough for two or three children at a time. There should be handholds for children to grab when they need to steady themselves. Wooden or plastic structures with different levels provide challenges for mobile infants, toddler, and twos. You can even fasten a steering wheel on one level.

Sandboxes—Mobile infants, toddlers, and twos have a wonderful time playing with sand outdoors, where you do not have to worry about a mess. You can purchase or make a sandbox or use a large tractor tire. Make sure you have a way of covering the sand to protect it from animals.

Water tubs—A table, trough, or tubs to hold water will delight children on hot days. Make sure that whatever you use can be emptied easily after each use. A hose, by itself or with a sprinkler, is another way to provide water play outdoors.

Tires—Automobile tires, embedded in the ground, become structures for mobile infants, toddlers, and twos. Children can climb into and out of them and sit for a while. Drill holes in the tires so that water cannot collect and become a breeding site for mosquitoes.

Playhouses, boats, and tunnels—You can purchase playhouses or construct them with the help of families. An old rowboat, sanded and painted, would be a great addition to the playground. Tunnels made from expandable wire covered with cloth can be stored easily when not in use.

Cardboard cartons—While not permanent structures, the cartons from computers and household appliances can be transformed into tunnels, playhouses, cars, or places for children to be alone for a while. Cut large windows and doors so that adults can see children at all times.

Selecting Materials and Experiences for Different Ages

The way young children use outdoor equipment and materials differs according to their temperaments, developmental levels, and previous experiences.

Young Infants

You need to be very near young infants, so one of the first considerations is to arrange places where you will be comfortable sitting with babies and where you can observe everything that is happening. To put infants down, you need a protected area where they can be safe from children who walk and run. In providing materials and experiences for young infants, think about what they will be doing outdoors.

Watching—If young infants are carried or placed where they can see what is happening outdoors, you have a natural playground for them. Babies can safely observe their surroundings from an infant carrier, stroller, infant swing, or infant seat. When they are comfortable, infants are eager to watch such things as blowing leaves, other children, and you. You can enhance the environment by hanging colorful scarves and other fabrics from trees or structures where they will be blown by the wind. Hanging crystals or colored pieces of Plexiglas® from a fence or tree branch will create interesting light patterns.

Listening—Outdoors, the noise of traffic, the chirping of crickets and birds, and the shouts of children at play will interest young infants. You can also place wind chimes outdoors where infants can hear them when the wind blows or when you gently strike them.

Reaching and grasping—Place some toys on a blanket for infants to grasp and explore. For ideas, see chapter 11, "Playing With Toys."

Moving and doing—Once infants can roll over and sit up, they need a flat, soft surface on which to move safely. They also need you to stay nearby.

Interacting—You are probably the most interesting part of the outdoor environment for young infants, just as you are interesting to them indoors. They will coo and respond as you talk about what is happening, sing to them, and draw their attention to interesting sights.

Mobile Infants

In addition to opportunities for sensory exploration, places for motor exploration are important for mobile infants. They crawl, pull up, cruise while holding onto structures or your hand, and soon walk. They still need a protected area where they will not be bumped by toddlers and twos who are moving quickly. Once mobile infants can walk on their own, run, and climb, they will want more freedom than an enclosed area allows, and your supervision will be critical to keeping them safe. To provide mobile infants with experiences they will enjoy, consider the kinds of activities that keep them busy and engaged.

Moving and exploring—Mobile infants need large enclosed spaces and places where they can climb, roll, slide, and swing safely. The structures described earlier will give them lots of appropriate challenges.

Pushing and pulling—Children who are just learning to walk enjoy sturdy toys that they can push and that help them keep their balance. Toy shopping carts and baby carriages are popular choices. Once they gain greater stability, they enjoy push-and-pull toys like toy lawn mowers and wagons.

Rolling and throwing—As discussed in chapter 11, "Playing With Toys," balls are probably the best toys for mobile infants. Outdoors, you can add the challenge of large balls like beach balls, soccer balls, and basketballs. Tightly sewn bean bags to throw into a basket are another option.

Collecting, dumping, and filling—This is a favorite activity of mobile infants, and it is easy to provide the materials they need. Small pails and buckets with handles are perfect for collecting small objects, including toys that you bring outdoors and natural materials like leaves, pinecones, and rocks. A lot of dumping and filling can take place in the sand area if you include small plastic shovels, rakes, scoops, small watering cans, plastic cups, and funnels. Remove any small items that could be choking hazards.

Playing with water—This is an especially nice way for mobile infants to cool off on a hot day. They can walk through a sprinkler, play with water from a hose, or play with water in a trough or dish pans. Add some plastic cups and a few scoops for an added challenge.

In addition to these common activities for mobile infants, you can set up special activities, such as blowing and chasing bubbles, painting with water and large brushes, or finger painting with shaving cream on a smooth surface.

Toddlers

In addition to the materials and experiences you plan for mobile infants, toddlers will enjoy the following additions.

More room for active play—Toddlers are on the move, and they want to use their large-muscle skills. They need plenty of open spaces to run, structures to climb on and jump from, opportunities to slide and build, and surfaces on which to ride wheeled toys.

Riding toys—A smooth surface with pathways is an ideal place for toddlers to use trucks and other riding toys that they can push with their feet.

More things to push and pull—Add wagons and wheelbarrows that toddlers can fill with objects and move. They may also like pushing dolls or stuffed animals in a doll carriage.

Construction materials—Another favorite activity of toddlers is building, knocking down, and building again. Large plastic blocks are a great addition for outdoor play, as are empty boxes and planks that they can walk along. If you have bales of hay, tires, and driftwood, toddlers will use these materials as part of their building projects.

Twos

Twos can really take advantage of their time outdoors when offered a number of choices. In addition to the experiences described for infants and toddlers, twos are ready for more complex and structured outdoor experiences.

Gardening—Twos can help you plant and care for a variety of flowers, herbs, and vegetables. It is best to start with plants rather than seeds, which take too long to sprout for even the most patient 2-year-old. They can help water the garden, check the plants each day for changes, help with the harvest, and enjoy the results.

Recommended Plants[51]

- Plants that attract butterflies: butterfly bushes, asters, dill, parsley, hollyhocks

- Plants that provide color, texture, scent and taste: lamb's ears, sage, mint, marigold, basil

- Fruits and vegetables that are easy to grow: cherry tomatoes, yellow pear tomatoes, peas, string beans, melons, carrots, broccoli

Observing animal life—Twos are fascinated by living things. Notice their excitement when they see birds, ants, squirrels, caterpillars, and worms. You can attract birds by putting feeders in the yard. Bug boxes enable twos to collect and study caterpillars or worms that they may be reluctant to hold. You can provide a magnifying glass for closer examinations. Be sure to set all creatures free before returning to the room.

Art materials—On occasion, bring out large colored chalk, brushes and paint, and playdough. The colors look even brighter outdoors, so the art experience is different.

Neighborhood walks—Think of areas in your community where children can visit. For example, the children would enjoy playing in a neighborhood park, taking a trip to the corner market, or walking down the street to a large tree to collect and run through the falling leaves.

Riding toys—In addition to the riding toys that toddlers use, older twos may be ready for small tricycles and vehicles that they can pedal. Be sure to provide helmets.

Ball games—Twos can run to a ball and kick it with increasing control. Always include some balls for them in the outdoor area. You can enhance their ball play by providing baskets to throw balls into and by playing catch and kickball with them.

Including All Children

The outdoor play space should ensure that children with disabilities can have the same or equivalent experiences as other children. You need to be aware of what interests each child and bring each child into the activities.

Many adaptations are simply a matter of common sense and are easy to accomplish. For example, a ramp can make it easier to get strollers and wheelchairs in and out of the building. Remove equipment that overturns easily if a child pulls herself up on it or leans heavily against it. Position a child with disabilities near other children so they can interact with each other.

Caring and Teaching

A particular challenge in taking infants, toddlers, and twos outdoors is the time it takes to get them ready, especially when the weather requires snowsuits, mittens, and boots. Try to keep in mind that dressing is a valuable activity, by itself, and not just something you have to do to take children outdoors. For ideas, see chapter 10, "Getting Dressed."

Meeting diapering and toileting needs when children are outdoors is another challenge. You must have a secluded area for diapering and toileting to protect children's privacy but, at the same time, you must maintain appropriate child-staff ratios. Some programs are fortunate enough to have a separate bathroom right off the play yard where a teacher can change a diaper or watch a child use the toilet while keeping an eye on what the other children are doing. If you have to go inside with a child, find out whether other children need to go as well. You can usually find a few toddlers and twos willing to go, so you will be able to take a small group with you, leaving other teachers to supervise the play yard. In many programs, several groups are outside at the same time, so more adults are supervising. You can also check and change diapers before going outdoors and make sure that children who use the toilet have had a chance to do so.

For walks, pack a shoulder bag or backpack with tissues, any special supplies for individual children, and a first-aid kit that contains emergency phone numbers and a cell phone or money for a pay phone. If you add a container of bubble-blowing solution, you will always have an engaging activity at hand.

It can be tempting for adults to think of going outdoors as taking a break from interacting with the children. While a change of scene is usually refreshing, children need you to remain on duty, observing, interacting, and sometimes playing with them. Children depend on you outdoors—just as they do indoors—to keep them safe and to respond in ways that make their experiences fun and meaningful.

Young Infants

Being outdoors offers young infants interesting sensory experiences.

> **Julio** (4 months) often falls asleep after a brief period of looking around.
>
> **Jasmine** (8 months) usually spends more time watching other children, sitting and playing on a blanket, swinging on a swing, and sitting on Janet's lap, reaching for objects that interest her.

To enhance children's pleasure and exploration, talk with them about what they are experiencing outdoors. Here are some examples of what you might say.

- Describe the experience: *It's a little cold outside today, isn't it? You are warm in your snowsuit and mittens, though.*
- Help them feel safe: *Here's a nice soft blanket for you to sit on. I'll sit right next to you.*
- Point out interesting sights: *Look how the wind is blowing the pretty fabric up and down, and up and down.*
- Enjoy interesting sounds together: *Do you hear the wind chimes?*

Mobile Infants

Mobile infants only need a little encouragement to take off outdoors, crawling, cruising, and climbing. Many like to join simple movement games. Almost all enjoy digging in the sand, playing with water, pushing wheeled toys, and dumping and filling containers.

> **Willard** (11 months) and **Abby** (14 months) love going outdoors. Each morning, Willard looks up eagerly when Grace asks if he is ready to go outside. Abby sometimes asks Brooks, "Uh?" and goes over to the stroller.

As you interact with mobile infants, you can enhance their enjoyment and learning by talking with them.

- Encourage appreciation and respect for nature: *Let's sit here. We can watch the squirrel climb the tree.*
- Promote feelings of competence: *You climbed up, all by yourself!*
- Describe and identify familiar sounds: *Crunch, crunch, crunch. The leaves crunch under your feet when you walk on them.*
- Verbalize feelings: *Uh, oh. That siren surprised you, didn't it?*
- Promote cooperative play: *Let's roll the ball to Lianna now.*

Toddlers and Twos

Leo, Matthew, Gena, Valisha, and Jonisha know what to expect when they go outdoors. They jump right into exploring and using the equipment and materials their teachers provide. Through their experiences, they are learning new vocabulary and concepts. Their developing gross- and fine-motor skills give them more control as they explore, and their developing cognitive and language skills support more complex play.

Close supervision is a major challenge when you take toddlers and twos outdoors. They can move quickly and climb, slide, and jump in a flash. Stay alert and try to anticipate what children will do so you can be prepared to step in when needed. Here are some ideas for providing special activities and challenges for children this age.

Play simple movement games. Invite children to flutter like butterflies, wiggle like worms, or pretend to be baby birds who fly away and come back to the nest. Show children how to make their shadows move. Play "Follow the Leader" and "Can You Do What I Do?"

Call attention to different sensations. Point out the rough bark on a tree, the soft leaf of a lamb's ear plant, the prickly pinecone, and the smooth rock. Call children's attention to how the air smells after a rain and to the smells of freshly cut grass and various flowers.

Invent games that promote the development of gross-motor skills. You can create a balancing path by laying boards or a piece of rope on the ground for children to walk along. Set up a bowling game where children try to knock down empty food boxes or plastic soda bottles by using a beach ball. Challenge twos to throw a beach ball into a laundry basket or large box. Invite children to chase bubbles that you blow.

Bring "indoor" materials outside. Encourage pretend play by placing props such as plastic vehicles, people, and animals in the sandbox. On warm days, bring books, musical instruments, and art materials outside for children to explore.

Enjoy the weather. You can still go outdoors when it is raining or snowing lightly. If the children are appropriately dressed, they will enjoy walking through puddles, catching snowflakes on their mittens, and making footprints in light snow. When the weather is too severe to go outdoors, bring some of the outdoors inside. Children can poke and dig in bins of snow or create a collage by sticking nontoxic leaves, twigs, and seeds on clear contact paper.

As always, interact with toddlers and twos outdoors in ways that support their development and learning.

- Introduce new words: *These silver maple seeds remind me of little helicopters. They spin around and around as they fall to the ground.*

- Follow children's interests: *Those ants are marching across the ground and going down those little holes. What do you think they are doing down there?*

- Encourage children to move and explore: *Let's see you jump like a grasshopper.*

- Ask open-ended questions: *What do you see? Where do you think that squirrel is going?*

- Stimulate imaginations: *What do you think the bird is saying when it chirps?*

Responding to and Planning for Each Child

As you observe children outdoors, think about the objectives for development and learning. Consider what each child is learning and how you might respond. Here is how three teachers who are implementing *The Creative Curriculum®* use what they learn from their observations to respond to each child and to plan.

Observe	Reflect	Respond
Jasmine (8 months) sits on a blanket on the playground, holding a flower. She looks at it closely, turning it in her hands. She brings the flower to her face and rubs it on her nose and cheek. She looks at Janet, babbles, and smiles.	Jasmine is noticing particular characteristics of objects (*Objective 11, Demonstrates positive approaches to learning; Dimension d, Shows curiosity and motivation*). She is using facial expressions and vocalizations to communicate (*Objective 9, Uses language to express thoughts and needs; Dimension a, Uses an expanding expressive vocabulary*).	Janet promotes Jasmine's language by responding, "Yes, I see that you have a yellow flower." She encourages Jasmine's examination of the flower by asking, "What does that flower smell like?" Janet leans over to smell the flower, inhaling deeply through her nose, to show Jasmine the meaning of her words.
Leo (18 months) walks around the park with Barbara and Donovan (16 months). Leo points to some fallen leaves and asks, "Dat?" He bends down, picks one up, and hands it to Barbara. She shows it to Donovan, who reaches out and touches it with his finger. Leo picks up another and hands it to Donovan. Donovan twirls the leaf in his hands. Leo picks up another and does the same.	Leo is having a brief play encounter with another child (*Objective 2, Establishes and sustains positive relationships; Dimension c, Interacts with peers*). He is imitating the actions of others (*Objective 14, Uses symbols and images to represent something not present; Dimension b, Engages in sociodramatic play*). He is using word-like sounds to communicate (*Objective 9, Uses language to express thoughts and needs; Dimension b, Speaks clearly*).	Barbara says, "Leo, you found some leaves," to model expressive language for him. She kneels down so that she is on the same level as the children. To support their play, she points to their leaves and describes what they are doing. "Donovan, Leo gave you a leaf. Now you each have one."

Observe	Reflect	Respond
Jonisha and Valisha (both 33 months) are bouncing a ball back and forth to each other on the playground. Valisha says, "I'm bouncing higher." "Me, too," Jonisha responds. "Ball goes higher and higher!" exclaims Valisha. Jonisha calls to LaToya, "Teacher, come see! Ball go so high!" Anton (32 months) stands near the girls, watching them. As LaToya approaches, Anton tugs at her sleeve, points at the girls, and says, "Me, too."	They are participating in coordinated play with each other (*Objective 2, Establishes and sustains positive relationships; Dimension c, Interacts with peers*). Jonisha and Valisha are participating in a conversation for two or more turns (*Objective 10, Uses appropriate conversational and other communication skills; Dimension a, Engages in conversations*).	LaToya acknowledges Jonisha's and Valisha's play. "Wow! You are bouncing that ball so high! You are also passing it back and forth to each other." LaToya wants to encourage the sisters to include others in their play. They frequently play together but not with other children. She says, "Anton is watching you pass that bouncy ball. I think he would like to bounce the ball with you."

Responsive Planning

In developing weekly plans, these teachers use their observations and refer to *Objectives for Development & Learning*. Here is what they record on their weekly planning forms.

- On the "Child Planning Form," under "Current Information," Janet writes about Jasmine's exploration of the flower. She decides to take her group on a walk the following week to the park where many flowers are blooming. She records this on her "Group Planning Form" as a special outdoor experience for Wednesday. Under "Family Involvement," she makes a note to ask for a volunteer to come with the group.

- As Barbara reads her observation notes about Leo, she realizes that he recently played briefly with other children. Three of those encounters involved dramatic play props. She records this on the "Child Planning Form" and makes a note under "Plans" to encourage such play encounters by adding a prop that a few children can use at the same time. On the "Group Planning Form," under "Changes to the Environment," she writes that she will add a three-seat steering bench to the pretend play props.

- LaToya has noticed that many of the children are engaging with each other for longer periods. She decides that she will add group mural painting, so she notes that on the "Group Planning Form" for Tuesday. She also writes a reminder to herself to get a roll of butcher paper from the supply room.

Make outdoor time a part of everyday life as you care for infants, toddlers and twos. You will enjoy the time you spend with them outside, and the benefits for the children will last a lifetime. The letter to families is one way to offer ideas about going outdoors with children.

Dear Families:

Going outdoors gives children an entirely different environment to explore. Outdoors, they can stretch their large muscles, breathe fresh air, take in the sunshine (or the rain or snow), and enjoy the freedom of open space. They can marvel at the creatures they find on the playground, watch the wind blow the trees, and collect seeds and stones. We try to take the children outdoors every day, because we know how important it is for their overall development and learning.

When your child does this…	**Your child is learning…**
• crawls through the grass	• to explore with all senses
• climbs over a tree stump	• to use gross-motor skills
• picks up pinecones to put in a bucket	• to group objects
• rolls a ball to another child	• social skills

What You Can Do at Home

Here are some activities to try next time you go outdoors with your child. You probably do some of them already. Perhaps others are new ideas.

- **Enjoy nature.** Talk about the breeze touching your cheeks. Roll down a grassy hill together. Plant a garden in your yard, a window box, or in a wheelbarrow that you can move as the sun moves. Take a bucket so your child can collect things such as stones and leaves. Be sure that the items do not present a choking hazard.

- **Take a texture walk.** Call your child's attention to natural materials and describe them. For example, you might point out *soft sand*, *rough pinecones*, and a *smooth rock.*

- **Invent games.** When your child walks well, create a balancing path by laying a piece of rope on the ground to walk along. Play a gentle game of catch. Set up a bowling game in which your child tries to knock down empty food boxes by rolling a beach ball.

- **Visit public playgrounds designed for children under age 3.** Playgrounds with equipment for very young children offer wonderful opportunities for children to practice their developing skills and to begin engaging with other children.

- **Take some "inside" activities outdoors.** For example, you might sit together under a tree and read a book. Give your child a paintbrush and water to paint the side of your house.

By working together, we can introduce your child to the joys and the wonders of the outdoors.

Sincerely,

References

[28] American Academy of Pediatrics & American Public Health Association. (2002). *Caring for our children: National health and safety performance standards: Guidelines for out-of-home care programs: A joint collaborative project of American Academy of Pediatrics, American Public Health Association, and National Resource Center for Health and Safety in Child Care* (2nd ed.). Elk Grove Village, IL: The Academy.

[29] Ibid.

[30] Ibid.

[31] National Institute of Child Health and Human Development. (2003, February). *Babies sleep safest on their backs* [NIH publication number 03-5355]. Bethesda, MD: National Institutes of Health.

[32] National Sleep Foundation. *Children's sleep habits.* Retrieved June 28, 2006, from http://www.Sleepfoundation.org/hottopics/index.php?secid=11&id=39

[33] Ibid.

[34] Ibid.

[35] American Academy of Pediatrics & American Public Health Association. (2002). *Caring for our children: National health and safety performance standards: Guidelines for out-of-home care programs: A joint collaborative project of American Academy of Pediatrics, American Public Health Association, and National Resource Center for Health and Safety in Child Care* (2nd ed.). Elk Grove Village, IL: The Academy.

[36] National Association for the Education of Young Children. (2005). Cleaning and sanitation frequency table. *NAEYC early childhood program standards and accreditation performance criteria.* Retrieved June 14, 2006, from http://www.naeyc.org/accreditation/criteria/sanitation.html

[37] Bronson, M. B. (1995). *The right stuff for children birth to 8: Selecting play materials to support development.* Washington, DC: National Association for the Education of Young Children.

[38] Assistive Technology Training Project. (1996). *Infusing assistive technology into early childhood classrooms.* Phoenix, AZ: Author.

[39] Nielsen, M., & Dissanayake, C. *Deferred imitation and the onset of pretend play in the second year.* Retrieved June 29, 2006, from http://www.warwick.ac.uk/fac/sci/Psychology/imitation/posters/m-nielsen.pdf

[40] Segal, M. (2004). The roots and fruits of pretending. In E. Zigler, D. G. Singer, & S. J. Bishop-Josef (Eds.), *Children's play: The roots of reading.* Washington, DC: ZERO TO THREE Press.

[41] Shonkoff, J. P., & Phillips, D. A. (Eds.). (2000). *From neurons to neighborhoods: The science of early childhood development*. Washington, DC: National Academy Press.

[42] Segal, M. (2004). The roots and fruits of pretending. In E. Zigler, D. G. Singer, & S. J. Bishop-Josef (Eds.), *Children's play: The roots of reading*. Washington, DC: ZERO TO THREE Press.

[43] Shonkoff, J. P., & Phillips, D. A. (Eds.). (2000). *From neurons to neighborhoods: The science of early childhood development*. Washington, DC: National Academy Press.

Ramsey, P. (1991). *Making friends in school: Promoting peer relationships in early childhood*. New York, NY: Teachers College Press.

[44] Segal, M. (2004). The roots and fruits of pretending. In E. Zigler, D. G. Singer, & S. J. Bishop-Josef (Eds.), *Children's play: The roots of reading*. Washington, DC: ZERO TO THREE Press.

[45] Hughes, F. (1999). *Children, play, and development* (3rd ed.). Boston, MA: Allyn and Bacon.

[46] Segal, M. (2004). The roots and fruits of pretending. In E. Zigler, D. G. Singer, & S. J. Bishop-Josef (Eds.), *Children's play: The roots of reading*. Washington, DC: ZERO TO THREE Press.

[47] Ibid.

[48] Cowley, J. (1999). *Mrs. Wishy-Washy*. New York, NY: Philomel Books.

[49] American Academy of Pediatrics & American Public Health Association. (2002). *Caring for our children: National health and safety performance standards: Guidelines for out-of-home care programs: A joint collaborative project of American Academy of Pediatrics, American Public Health Association, and National Resource Center for Health and Safety in Child Care* (2nd ed.). Elk Grove Village, IL: The Academy.

[50] From *Caring for our Children: National Health and Safety Performance Standards: Guidelines for Out-of-Home Child Care Programs: A Joint Collaborative Project of American Academy of Pediatrics, American Public Health Association, and National Resource Center for Health and Safety in Child Care* (2nd ed.) (p. 263), by American Academy of Pediatrics and American Public Health Association, 2002, Elk Grove Village, IL: The Academy. Copyright 2002 by AAP, APA, and NRCHSCC. Reprinted with permission.

[51] Torquati, J., & Barber, J. (2005). Dancing with trees: Infants and toddlers in the garden. *Young Children, 60*(3), 43.

General Resources

Baker, A., & Manfredi-Petitt, L. (2004). *Relationships, the heart of quality care: Creating community among adults in early care settings.* Washington, DC: National Association for the Education of Young Children.

Bardige, B. (2005). *At a loss for words: How America is failing our children and what we can do about it.* Philadelphia, PA: Temple University Press.

Bardige, B., & Segal, M. (2005). *Building literacy with love: A guide for teachers and caregivers of children birth through age 5,* Washington, DC: ZERO TO THREE Press.

Berk, L. (2004). *Infants and children: Prenatal through middle childhood.* Needham Heights, MA: Allyn & Bacon.

Brazelton, T. B. (1992). *Touchpoints birth to three: The essential reference for the early years.* Cambridge, MA: Da Capo Press.

Brilliant Beginnings, LLC. (1999). *Baby brain basics guidebook: Birth to 12 months.* Long Beach, CA: Author.

Carlson, V., Feng, X., & Harwood, R. (2004). The "ideal baby": A look at the intersection of temperament and culture. *Zero to Three, 24*(4), 22–28.

Day, M., & Parlakian, R. (2004). *How culture shapes social-emotional development: Implications for practice in infant-family programs.* Washington, DC: ZERO TO THREE Press.

Egeland, B., & Erickson, M. (1999). *Attachment theory and research.* Retrieved June 30, 2005, from http://www.zerotothree.org/vol20-2.html

Ezell, H. K., & Justice, L. M. (2005). *Shared storybook reading: Building young children's language and emergent literacy skills.* Baltimore, Maryland: Paul H. Brookes Publishing Co.

Gonzalez-Mena, J. (2005). *Diversity in early care and education: Honoring differences.* New York, NY: McGraw-Hill.

Greenman, J. (2005). *Caring spaces, learning places: Children's environments that work.* Redmond, WA: Exchange Press, Inc.

Greenman, J., & Stonehouse, A. (1996). *Prime times: A handbook for excellence in infant and toddler programs.* St. Paul, MN: Redleaf Press.

Grotberg, E. (1995). *A guide to promoting resilience in children: Strengthening the human spirit.* Retrieved June 30, 2005, from http://resilnet.uiuc.edu/library/grotb95b.html

Hart, B., & Risley, T. R. (1999). *The social world of children learning to talk.* Baltimore, MD: Paul H. Brookes Publishing Co., Inc.

Honig, A. (2002). *Secure relationships: Nurturing infant/toddler attachment in early care settings.* Washington, DC: National Association for the Education of Young Children.

Howes, C. & Ritchie, S. (2002). *A matter of trust: Connecting teachers and learners in the early childhood classroom.* New York, NY: Teachers College Press.

Jalongo, M. R. (2004). *Young children and picture books.* Washington, DC: National Association for the Education of Young Children.

Kohl, M. F. (2002). *First art: Art experiences for toddlers and twos.* Beltsville, MD: Gryphon House, Inc.

Lally, J. R., Griffin, A., Fenichel, E., Segal, M., Szanton, E., & Weissbourd, B. (2003). *Caring for infants and toddlers in groups: Developmentally appropriate practice.* Washington, DC: ZERO TO THREE Press.

Lally, J. R., & Mangione, P. (2006, July). The uniqueness of infancy demands a responsive approach to care. *Young Children, 61*(4), 14–20.

Lerner, C., & Dombro, A. (2000). *Learning and growing together: Understanding and supporting your child's development.* Washington, DC: ZERO TO THREE Press.

Miché, M. (2002). *Weaving music into young minds.* Albany, NY: Delmar.

Miller, K. (2000). *Things to do with toddlers and twos* (Revised ed.). Beltsville, MD: TelShare Publishing Co., Inc.

Neuman, S. B., & Dickinson, D. K. (Eds.). (2002). *Handbook of early literacy research.* New York, NY: The Guilford Press.

Olds, A. R. (2001). *Child care design guide.* New York, NY: McGraw-Hill.

Oser, C., & Cohen, J. (2003). *America's babies: The ZERO TO THREE Policy Center data book.* Washington, DC: ZERO TO THREE Press.

Pica, R. (2004). *Experiences in movement: Birth to age 8* (3rd ed.). Clifton Park, NY: Delmar Learning.

Raines, S., Miller, K., & Curry-Rood, L. (2002). *Story stretchers for infants, toddlers, and twos: Experiences, activities, and games for popular children's books.* Beltsville, MD: Gryphon House.

Sawyer, W. E. (2004). *Growing up with literature.* Clifton Park, NY: Delmar Learning.

Segal, M. (1998). *Your child at play: Birth to one year* (2nd ed.). New York, NY: Newmarket Press.

Shore, R. (1997). *Rethinking the brain: New insights into early development.* New York, NY: Families and Work Institute.

Torelli, L., & Durrett, C. (1998). *Landscapes for learning: Designing group care environments for infants, toddlers and two-year-olds.* Berkeley, CA: Torelli/Durrett Infant & Toddler Child Care Furniture.

U. S. Department of Health and Human Services, Administration for Children and Families, Administration on Children, Youth and Families, Head Start Bureau, Head Start Facilities. (2000). *Head Start center design guide.* Washington, DC: Author.